MONOLOGUES from CONTEMPORARY LITERATURE
Volume I

ERIC KRAUS is the co-founder of Smith and Kraus, Inc. He is also the editor of <u>The Great Monologues from the Humana Festival</u>.

JACK O'BRIEN is the Artistic Director of the Old Globe Theatre in San Diego, California.

Other Books for Actors from Smith and Kraus

The Best Men's Stage Monologues of 1990

The Best Women's Stage Monologues of 1990

Street Talk: Character Monologues for Actors

Great Scenes for Young Actors From the Stage

The Best Stage Scenes for Men from the 1980's

The Best Stage Scenes for Women from the 1980's

One Hundred Men's Stage Monologues from the 1980's

One Hundred Women's Stage Monologues from the 1980's

The Great Monologues from the Humana Festival

The Best Men's Stage Monologues of 1991

The Best Women's Stage Monologues of 1991

Great Monologues for Young Actors

The Great Monologues from the EST Marathon

If you require pre-publication information about upcoming Smith and Kraus monologue collections, scene collections, technique books and directories, you may receive our semi-annual catalogue, free of charge, by sending your name and address to Smith and Kraus Catalogue, P.O. Box 10, Newbury, VT 05051.

MONOLOGUES from CONTEMPORARY LITERATURE
Volume I

Edited by
Eric Kraus

The Monologue Audition Series

SK
A Smith and Kraus Book

Cover and text design by Jeannette Champagne

Manufactured in the United States of America

First Edition: June 1992
10 9 8 7 6 5 4 3 2

Cataloging in Publication
(Prepared by Quality Books, Inc.)

Monologues from contemporary literature, volume I / edited by Eric Kraus.
p. cm. -- (The monologue audition series)
Preassigned LCCN: 92-64133.
Includes bibliographical references.
ISBN 1-880399-04-0

1. Monologues. 2. Acting. I. Kraus, Eric, 1936-

PN2080.M544 1992   792'.028
                        QBI92-1076

Smith and Kraus, Inc.
Main Street, P.O. Box 10, Newbury, Vermont 05051
(802) 866-5423

ACKNOWLEDGMENTS

Great appreciation to the authors and to Jeffrey Kraus.

CONTENTS

CONTENTS

<u>Monologues for Women:</u>

CONTENTS

PUBLISHER'S NOTE

In order to preserve the material's integrity, we have reprinted the text from which each monologue is taken in its entirety, as it appears in the original published work.

All text that is not part of the actual monologue has been put in brackets and italicized for your convenience.

INTRODUCTION

I wonder if there is a professional anywhere, "on either side to the desk," who doesn't resent the humiliation called "auditioning." The mere fact of someone who earns his or her living in the theatre, walking into a strange room to face one, two, or even a panel of passive, seemingly disinterested, and apparently rude people in the hopes of securing a job with only about two or three minutes of allotted attention would make the Spanish Inquisition a mere "comb-out" by comparison.

And each time I grit my teeth to face the process, I remind myself that not only has this been going on since Sophocles strapped on his sandals, but there is probably something inherently correct about it. I mean, isn't the point of entertainment to be "grabbed," to be stopped or arrested by the quality, the energy, the intelligence, the "something" of a performer? Didn't our thespian ancestors stand by the side of the road, juggling for the passing King, in hopes of catching his eye, then his interest, and perhaps subsequently even his heart? It never occurred to them to ask to "take a lunch" with His Majesty. First they had to get his attention.

In a world currently comprised of "sound bytes," we should be able to acknowledge what is honest about this seemingly inhuman process, and bring our best shot to it. It is probably always worth noting and remembering that the person for whom you are preparing the audition is truly rooting for you. Those of us in the habit of hiring actors want to be knocked out; we want the person walking through the door to be just exactly what we were looking for. And in the immortal words of Cocteau, we genuinely long to be "astonished."

Well, in my experience, the best way to go about that is probably to be found in this volume, or others like it. The best auditions I have ever seen have been those with material so fresh, so new, so uncommon that I was forced to listen, and once I found myself really listening, I was captured. Sometimes I think if I see one more actor clear his throat and begin "Thou, Nature, art my goddess..." I'll jump through the nearest window. (Which might

INTRODUCTION

well be the goal of my next auditionee!) But when I pause at the conclusion of an audition and ask "What <u>was</u> that?" the person facing me knows well that they have reached well past fatigue, past indifference, past the stale air in that particular room and have struck the responsive chord that is what we're both looking for.

You can see it in the eyes of those on the other side of that dreaded desk. "I see you," they seem to say. "I recognize you." And the next words are then bound to be "I like you, and dammit, I'm going to hire you."

The sweetest phrase in the English theatrical vocabulary.

—Jack O'Brien
Artistic Director
the Old Globe Theatre

MONOLOGUES from
CONTEMPORARY
LITERATURE
Volume I

AGE OF IRON
by J.M. Coetzee
South Africa - Present - Mrs. Curran (60's)

Mrs. Curran, a widow sick with cancer, tells a 12-year-old black activist who is just returning from a stay in the hospital about the realities of his situation and the fate of his compatriot.

MRS. CURRAN: I want to speak to you seriously, [*I said.*] You are too young for this kind of thing. I told Bheki so and I tell you again. You must listen to me. I am an old person, I know what I am talking about. You are still children. You are throwing away your lives before you know what life can be. What are you—fifteen years old? Fifteen is too young to die. Eighteen is too young. Twenty-one is too young.

[*He got up, brushing the red band with his fingertips. A favor. In the age of chivalry men hacked other men to death with women's favors fluttering on their helmets. A waste of breath to preach prudence to this boy. The instinct for battle too strong in him, driving him on. Battle: nature's way of liquidating the weak and providing mates for the strong. Return covered in glory, and you shall have your desire. Gore and glory, death and sex. And I, an old woman, crone of death, tying a favor around his head!*]

[*Where is Bheki? he said.*]

[*I searched his face. Had he not understood what I told him? Had he forgotten?*] Sit down, [*I said.*]

[*He sat.*]

[*I leaned across the table.*] Bheki is in the ground, [*I said.*] He is in a box in a hole with earth heaped on top of him. He is never going to leave that hole. Never, never, never. Understand: this is not a game like football, where after you fall down you get up and go on playing. The men you are playing against don't say to each other, 'That one is just a child, let us shoot a child's bullet at him, a play bullet.' They don't think of you as a child at all. They think of you as the enemy and they hate you quite as much as you hate them. They will have no qualms about shooting you; on the

1

contrary, they will smile with pleasure when you fall and make another notch on their gunstocks.

[*He stared back at me as if I were striking him in the face, blow after blow. But, jaw set, lips clenched, he refused to wince. Over his eyes that smoky film.*]

You think their discipline is poor, [*I said.*] You are wrong. Their discipline is very good. What holds them back from exterminating every male child, every last one of you, is not compassion or fellow feeling. It is discipline, nothing else: orders from above, that can change any day. Compassion is flown out of the window. This is war. Listen to what I am saying! I know what I am talking about. You think I am trying to lure you out of the struggle. Well, that is true. That is what I am doing. I say: Wait, you are too young.

[*He shifted restlessly. Talk, talk! Talk had weighed down the generations of his grandparents and the generations of his parents. Lies, promises, blandishments, threats: they had walked stooped under the weight of all the talk. Not he. He threw off talk. Death to talk!*]

You say it is time to fight, [*I said.*] You say it is time to win or lose. Let me tell you something about that *win or lose*. Let me tell you something about that *or*. Listen to me.

You know I am sick. Do you know what is wrong with me? I have cancer. I have cancer from the accumulation of shame I have endured in my life. That is how cancer comes about: from self-loathing the body turns malignant and begins to eat away at itself.

You say, 'What is the point of consuming yourself in shame and loathing? I don't want to listen to the story of how you feel, it is just another story, why don't you *do* something?' And when you say that, I say, 'Yes.' I say, 'Yes.' I say, 'Yes.'

There is nothing I can reply but 'Yes' when you put that question to me. But let me tell you what it is like to utter that 'Yes.' It is like being on trial for your life and being allowed only two words, Yes and No. Whenever you take a breath to speak out, you

2

re warned by the judges: 'Yes or No: no speeches.' 'Yes,' you
say. Yet all the time you feel other words stirring inside you like
life in the womb. Not like a child kicking, not yet, but like the very
beginnings, like the deepdown stirring of knowledge a woman has
when she is pregnant.

There is not only death inside me. There is life too. The death
is strong, the life is weak. But my duty is to the life. I must keep
it alive. I must.

You do not believe in words. You think only blows are real,
blows and bullets. But listen to me: can't you hear that the words
I speak are real? Listen! They may only be air but they come from
my heart, from my womb. They are not Yes, they are not No.
What is living inside me is something else, another word. And I am
fighting for it, in my manner, fighting for it not to be stifled. I am
like one of those Chinese mothers who know that their child will be
taken away from them, if it is a daughter, and done away with,
because the need, the family's need, the village's need, is for sons
with strong arms. They know that after the birth someone will come
into the room, someone whose face will be hidden, who will take the
child from the midwife's arms and, if the sex is wrong, turn his back
on them, out of delicacy, and stifle it just like that, pinching the little
nose to, holding the jaw shut. A minute and all is done.

Grieve if you like, the mother is told afterward: grief is only
natural. But do not ask: What is this thing called a son? What is
this thing called a daughter, that it must die?

Do not misunderstand me. You are a son, somebody's son. I
am not against sons. But have you ever seen a newborn baby? Let
me tell you, you would find it hard to tell the difference between
boy and girl. Every baby has the same puffy-looking fold between
the legs. The spout, the tendril that is said to mark out the boy is no
great thing, really. Very little to make the difference between life
and death. Yet everything else, everything indefinite, everything
that gives when you press it, is condemned unheard. I am arguing
for that unheard.

3

AGE OF IRON

You are tired of listening to old people, I can see. You are itching to be a man and do a man's things. You are tired of getting ready for life. It is time for life itself, you think. What an error you are making! Life is not following a stick, a pole, a flagstaff, a gun, and seeing where it will take you. Life is not around the corner. You are already in the midst of life.

THE BEAN TREES
by Barbara Kingsolver
Arizona - Present - Taylor (20's)

Taylor tries to console Esperanza, a Mexican who can barely understand English and who has lost her child.

TAYLOR: Esperanza, [*I said, and she nodded toward a door at the back.*]

[*That room seemed to belong in another house—it was empty. The walls were an antique-looking shade of light pink, completely bare except for a cross with two palm fronds stuck behind it, over one of the beds. The two beds were neatly made up with rough-looking blue blankets that surely no one would sleep under in this weather. Esperanza was not in either bed, but sitting up in a straight-backed chair by the window. She looked up when I knocked on the door casement.*]

Hi, I came to see how you were doing.

[*She got up from the chair and offered it to me. She sat on the bed. I don't believe she had been doing anything at all, just sitting with her hands in her lap.*]

[*We looked at each other for a second, then looked at other things in the room, of which there were painfully few. I didn't know why I'd thought I'd have the nerve to do this.*]

How are you feeling now? Are you feeling better? Your stomach's okay? [*I put my hand on my stomach. Esperanza nodded, then looked at her hands.*]

[*I had lost my directions somewhere when I came into the house. I looked out the window expecting to see Roosevelt Park, but this was not that window. We were at the back of the house. From here you got a terrific birds-eye view of Lee Sing's back garden. I wondered if you might catch a peek at Lee Sing's old mother from up here, if you stayed at your post long enough.*]

I've been meaning to tell you, [*I said,*] I think Esperanza's a beautiful name. Estevan told me it means to wait, and also to hope. That in Spanish the same word means both things. But I thought it was pretty even before I knew it meant anything. It reminded me of, I don't know, a waterfall or something.

[*She nodded.*]

Taylor doesn't mean anything that interesting. A tailor hems up people's pants and stuff like that.

[*Her mouth stretched a little bit in the direction of a smile. But her eyes looked blank. Dark, black holes.*]

You understand basically everything I'm saying, right?

[*She nodded again.*]

I think that's how Turtle is, too, but people always forget. They think she doesn't take in any more than she puts out, but I know better, I can tell she understands stuff. It's something about the way she looks at you.

[*Esperanza kept staring at her empty hands. I wished I had something to put in them, something that would be wonderful for her to look at.*]

I hope you don't mind me talking about Turtle.

[*Her eyes flew up at me like a pair of blackbirds scared out of safe hiding.*]

Estevan told me about Ismene, [*I said.*] I'm sorry. When I first found out you'd taken pills, I couldn't understand it, why you'd do such a thing to yourself. To Estevan. But when he told me that, God, how does a person live with something like that?

[*She looked away. This conversation would have been hard enough even with two people talking. No matter what I said, it was sure to be the exact wrong thing to say to someone who recently swallowed a bottle of baby aspirin. But what would be right? Was there some book in the library where you could look up such things?*]

I guess the main thing I came up here to tell you is, I don't know how you go on, but I really hope you'll keep doing it. That you won't give up *esperanza*. I thought of that last night. *Esperanza* is all you get, no second chances. What you have to do is try and think of reasons to stick it out.

THE BEAN TREES

[*She had tears in her eyes, but that seemed better somehow than nothing at all.*] It's terrible to lose somebody, [*I said.*] I mean, I don't know firsthand, but I can imagine it must be. But it's also true that some people never have anybody to lose, and I think that's got to be so much worse.

THE BEAN TREES
by Barbara Kingsolver
Arizona - Present - Lou Ann (20's)

Here, Lou Ann describes a job interview she has just come from at a convenience store.

LOU ANN: So the first thing the guy says to me is 'We get a lot of armed robberies in here, sweetheart.' He kept on calling me sweetheart and talking to my boobs instead of my face, this big flabby guy with greasy hair and you just know he reads every one of those porno magazines they keep behind the counter. 'Lots of stickups, sweetheart, how do you hold up under pressure?' he says. Holdup, that was his idea of a big hilarious joke. Jeez, the whole thing gave me the creeps from the word go.

THE BEAN TREES
by Barbara Kingsolver
Arizona - Present - Taylor (20's)

Taylor's daughter, Turtle, has just been molested. Here, Taylor is weeping as she explains the depth of her upset to her friend Lou Ann.

TAYLOR: I don't know where to start, Lou Ann, [*I told her.*] There's just so damn much ugliness. Everywhere you look, some big guy kicking some little person when they're down—look what they do to those people at Mattie's. To hell with them, people say, let them die, it was their fault in the first place for being poor or in trouble, or for not being white, or whatever, how dare they try to come to this country.

[*I thought you were upset about Turtle, Lou Ann said.*]

[*About Turtle, sure. I looked out the window.*] But it just goes on and on, there's no end to it. [*I didn't know how to explain the empty despair I felt.*] How can I just be upset about Turtle, about a grown man hurting a baby, when the whole way of the world is to pick on people that can't fight back?

[*You fight back, Taylor. Nobody picks on you and lives to tell the tale.*]

[*I ignored this.*] Look at those guys out in the park with no place to go, [*I said.*] And women, too. I've seen whole families out there. While we're in here trying to keep the dry-cleaner bags out of the kids' reach, those mothers are using dry-cleaner bags for their children's *clothes,* for God's sake. For raincoats. And feeding them out of the McDonald's dumpster. You'd think that life alone would be punishment enough for those people, but then the cops come around waking them up mornings, knocking them around with their sticks. You've seen it. And everybody else saying hooray, way to go, I got mine, power to the toughest. Clean up the neighborhood and devil take the riffraff.

[*Lou Ann just listened.*]

What I'm saying is nobody feels sorry for anybody anymore,

nobody even pretends they do. Not even the President. It's like it's become unpatriotic. [*I unfolded my wad of handkerchief and blew my nose.*]

What's that supposed to teach people? [*I demanded.*] It's no wonder kids get the hurting end of the stick. And she's so little, so many years ahead of her. I'm just not up to the job, Lou Ann.

BECAUSE IT IS BITTER, AND BECAUSE IT IS MY HEART
by Joyce Carol Oates
Hammond, NY - Present - Persia (31)

Persia has gone to the studio of her brother-in-law Leslie to be photographed with her daughter Iris. A thunderstorm and blackout traps them there. They drink and Persia gets drunk. She talks about life and her unsatisfactory relationship with her husband.

PERSIA: In a flash of lightning it's as if your skull is pried open, isn't it? And you're spilled out, somehow? Not you-who-you-are but you-inside-of-you. As if the world is ending and you see how... silly you've been, and petty, and small-minded, and stupid, thinking the wrong things mattered, all along. Does that make sense? [*She laughs nervously, yet is pleased with her words. She is a woman whom men have so often flattered with their attentiveness to her words, such pleasure comes as a reflex.*]

[*Leslie has been staring at her. What? Does what make sense?*]
I must be drunk.

[*No, you're not.*]
I'm *not*, I can't be. I've only had...I haven't had much. [*She watches Iris passing through a room, two doorways away, a long-legged child, headstrong, secretive, with a look of deep hurt.... Why hadn't Persia had a second baby, before it was too late? She says carefully,*] This rain! It's like we're inside Niagara Falls. Washing everything away...all the dirt. [*There is a long pause. A lightning flash, and a beat of several seconds, and resounding thunder...the electrical storm at the heart of the rainstorm is moving to the east. She says in a lowered voice, suddenly urgent,*] It's true, what he told you. I was the one who asked him to leave. So that I could think. So that I wouldn't always just...feel. [*She adds bitterly,*] Duke has that effect upon women. He counts on it.

[*Does he!, Leslie murmurs.*]

[*Persia says,*] When I found out he'd betrayed me, gone outside the marriage—

11

BECAUSE IT IS BITTER, AND BECAUSE IT IS MY HEART

[*Betrayed you? How do you mean?, Leslie asks. Not with other women?*]

In different ways, [*Persia says quickly.*] I don't want to go into details. If you love and trust someone he can betray you with a word...an expression on his face. You know. Or maybe, [*she says carelessly,*] you don't know.

[*Well, says Leslie, smiling at his long bony fingers, that's possible.*]

When I first found out, I was almost happy...the way you are when something has been decided for you. Because when you love another person there is something off-center in you, like, you know, your soul is partly inside that person; it's been drawn out of you and it's in someone else? and might be injured? And you can't know, you really can't know, if it won't be? My parents are just farm people I guess you would say—I mean, Duke *did* say—simple people I suppose, they're Methodists, and they believe in Jesus Christ as their redeemer, and that sort of thing, but if you asked them to explain or to analyze, the way Duke analyzes things, to shed a little light on the subject, as Duke says, they'd clam up...they'd be embarrassed and resentful. Because there are things you don't talk about. Because there aren't the words. And falling in love with someone so different from yourself and anyone you know—getting married, having a baby, starting a family, living, you know, an adult life, living what you believe to be an adult life, a real life—nobody talks about these things, nobody seems to know the words. Like dancing, and suddenly the old steps aren't there for you, or the beat is wrong, so you have to improvise. [*She speaks quickly, half angrily, lifting her hair from the nape of her neck and fanning it out and letting it fall several times, not knowing what she does.*]

[*But you love him, Leslie says softly.*]

But I can't live with him, [*Persia says. She smiles, she's triumphant.*] I won't.

BECAUSE IT IS BITTER, AND BECAUSE IT IS MY HEART
by Joyce Carol Oates
Hammond, NY - Present - Sugar Baby Fairchild (20's)

Sugar Baby tries to convince his kid brother Jinx to shave points
in an upcoming championship-round basketball game.

SUGAR BABY: Ain't nobody said anything about *losin'* any fuckin'
game, boy, you readin' me wrong—you just don't play so cool, is
all. A game is won by two points like it's won by twenty. It's the
point spread that's the thing, and Iceman surely got his off nights
like anybody else. Shit, there's Ernie Banks hisself, he was a rookie
with the Cubs...I bet you Babe Ruth, Stan Musial, all of 'em. Jinx
Fairchild the coolest player these shitheads ever seen, so, comes this
night, over at Troy, maybe your team's kind of nerved up, scared,
maybe Iceman has got a nasty cough, don't have to do any asshole
thing, boy, any actual mistake, you just ain't so cool is all. And
nobody's goin' to know 'cause who can read minds?

[*Sugar Baby is shooting baskets with Jinx, cigarette in his
mouth: if he sinks one, OK; if he misses doesn't give a shit, ain't
nothing but a boys' game anyway.*]

[*Seeing his brother's face so stiff and his eyes hooded and hurt,
Sugar Baby continues, laying a hand on Jinx's shoulder that Jinx
shrugs off,*] I was watchin' you once, boy, you's just a kid, in the
house; you knocked this glass or somethin' off the table with your
elbow, then, right in midair, before it crash, you catch it. Jesus,
just reach around and catch it! Like it wasn't anything you thought
about 'cause can't nobody think that fast, just somethin' you done,
like a cat swats a moth. I'm fast too, and I got eyes around the side
of my head too, but I ain't like that...that's *weird.* So what I'm
sayin', boy, is you got reflexes you don't even think about, so any
time you start thinkin' about them maybe you're goin' to be slowed
up some, which would make you the speed of any other asshole
playin' past his capacity, and in the game, that night, seein' it's the
semifinals and Troy ain't that bad and all Hammond's got is mainly
you and that big clodhopper guard what's-his-name...so Iceman

13

naturally goin' to be thinkin' more than just some ordinary game, right? Tryin' real hard to win the championship for all them whiteys, right? Fuck-face Breuer jumpin' up and down like he's comin' in his pants, right? Well, maybe, that night, performin' monkey just ain't so *cool,* is all. It's natural. Ain't nobody goin' to blame you, you do it smooth. And you so smooth anyhow, boy, you can fuck up and look good at the same time. Say there's some asshole gets open, and you know, you pass him the ball, he prob'ly ain't goin' to score, but you pass him the ball anyhow maybe bouncin' it sort of wrong and he loses it...or you got a free throw and get coughin'...any kind of shit like that. Like I say, two points can win a game like twenty...or whatever. Long as you win. Ain't that so, baby?

[*It's a cool sunny wind-whisked April morning, Jinx Fairchild bareheaded in soiled work pants and T-shirt, Sugar Baby Fairchild a sight for the eyes in new maroon cord trousers with a wide leather brass-buckled belt (initials SBF in script), antelope-hide jacket, two-inch-heeled square-toed kidskin boots, four-inch-brimmed velour hat pushed to the side back of his head...meticulously trimmed sideburns, mustache...the whites of his eyes eerily white as he speaks, as if for emphasis. The quieter Jinx Fairchild is, the more Sugar Baby Fairchild talks. It's like singing, his talk, like humming: the same words used again and again till they almost aren't words but just sounds, a comfort to them*].

[*No secret in the neighborhood that Sugar Baby Fairchild is Poppa D.'s newest young man; even Minnie Fairchild must know her boy has got some tight connection with Leo Lyman over in Buffalo... Leo Lyman who's so legendary a name among local blacks. And there's the 1956 Eldorado, gleaming pink and gold, chrome like bared grinning teeth, and all the accessories, and the fancy apartment on Genesee Street where he's living with this good-looking high-yalla woman who's an old friend too of Poppa D.'s*].

[*Seem like everybody, in a certain circle, is tight friends of everybody else.*]

BECAUSE IT IS BITTER, AND BECAUSE IT IS MY HEART

[*These days, Sugar Baby Fairchild isn't welcome in the house on East Avenue; Minnie won't have him. Won't even accept money from him, or presents. The few times he has offered*].

[*Sugar Baby Fairchild has told his family it's privileged work he does for Poppa D....whole lot better than janitor work or shoveling gravel or cleaning up white folks' shit at the hospital or some hotel uptown or hauling away their garbage, which is what his friends from high school do, mostly. He doesn't see Jinx very often, runs into him on the street sometimes; this is the first time he has actually sought Jinx out, approaching him in the playground where Jinx is practicing baskets, and at first it isn't clear to Jinx what Sugar Baby wants, why he's so friendly, so interested in Jinx's plans for the future...this is the brother who hadn't troubled to attend one of Jinx Fairchild's games this year*].

[*And in those clothes, tight pants and high-heeled shoes, and smoking a cigarette, Sugar Baby surely isn't interested in fooling around with a basketball.*]

[*Now Jinx knows what it is, Jinx isn't saying anything. His legs stiff like a zombie or robot in a movie and he's missing half his shots...and Sugar Baby's getting impatient, working up a little sweat.*] Shit, you actin' like some gal thinks her pussy's so special can't nobody touch it. What you care about them white mothas? You think they care about *you*? You think they give a shit about you? All you is, boy, is a performin' monkey for them, same as I was, and if you don't perform, you on your ass...and they turn their attention to the next monkey. You think they give a shit about *you*? Truth is, asshole, they don't even know *you*: never heard of *you*.

BECAUSE IT IS BITTER, AND BECAUSE IT IS MY HEART
by Joyce Carol Oates
Hammond, NY - Present - Persia Courtney (30's)

Persia, a deteriorating alcoholic, reacts to her daughter Iris'
efforts to help her stop drinking.

PERSIA: How dare you? *You!* Have you nothing better to do with
your time than spy on me? [*Persia cries, furious when, after days
of hesitating, Iris finally brings up the subject of Persia's drinking.*]
My own daughter spying...like every busybody and asshole in this
neighborhood. Are *you* so perfect?... Little Miss Honor Roll!...
Little Miss Smart-Ass!...I do what I do and what I damn well want
to do....I deserve some happiness....*I'm* the one who pays the bills
around here—on my feet every night at that damned place required
to smile at every son of a bitch who comes in, pinches my rear,
sometimes the bastard will squeeze my breasts...what you do then is
smile, sugar, smile, *smile, SMILE,* 'cause if you don't you're out on
your ass—what do *you* know about it?...Such disrespect...such selfishness...Little Miss Perfect!...If I hear you're spreading tales of me,
to Maddy or Les or any of my friends, or to your goddamned father
—*especially him*—I'll slap your mean little face so hard you won't
know what hit you....My own daughter...spying on me...after all
I've sacrificed for you...*after all I've sacrificed for you you little
bitch!*

16

THE BOOK OF SAINTS
by Nino Ricci
Italy - 1960 - Grandfather (60's)

Grandpa responds to his daughter, who is pregnant but not by her husband, who is in America.

GRANDPA: For *my* sake! Was it for my sake you behaved like a common whore? Do you think you're better than those people? *They* are my people, not you, not someone who could do what you've done. I've suffered every day of my life, *per l'amore di Cristo,* but I've never had to walk through this town and hang my head in shame. Now people come to my house like they go to the circus, to laugh at the clowns! You've killed me, Cristina, you killed your mother when you were born and now you've killed me, as surely as if you'd pulled a knife across my throat. In all my days I've never raised a hand against you but now I wish to God I'd locked you in the stable and raised you with the pigs, that you'd died and rotted in the womb, that you hadn't lived long enough to bring this disgrace on my name!

THE BOOK OF SAINTS
by Nino Ricci
Italy - 1960 - Cristina (30ish)

Cristina is leaving Italy for America. She has been given the
"evil eye" by the villagers for being pregnant out of wedlock.
She speaks to the people as she leaves.

CRISTINA: Fools! [*she shouted now*.] You tried to kill me but
you see I'm still alive. And now you came to watch me hang, but
I won't be hanged, not by your stupid rules and superstitions. You
are the ones who are dead, not me, because not one of you knows
what it means to be free and to make a choice, and I pray to God
that he wipes this town and all its stupidities off the face of the
earth!

BOSS OF BOSSES
by Joseph F. O'Brien and Andris Kurins
New York City - Present - Joseph Gallo (60's)

Joe, consigliere to the Godfather, is depressed that one of their
people is in the hands of the FBI and may talk. He speaks to
the Godfather.

JOE: Iannuzzi's the problem, [*said the consigliere.*]
   [*Iannuzzi's in the loving hands of the feds, said the Godfather.
Who's gonna take the contract? You?*]
   [*Again there was a silence, but now it seemed to the listening
agents that it was the befuddled quiet of two old men who were
powerless to act.*]
   It's all turning to shit, isn't it? [*said Joe Gallo.*]
   [*The Godfather said nothing.*]
   I mean, you spend your life working on this thing, this thing of
ours. You think you're doing right. Then something happens,
something goes off track, you get old, it don't look like it used to
look. Disappointed. You end up disappointed. And the bitch of it
is, you can't put your finger on what went wrong. You're doing
good, you're doing good, you're doing good. But somehow, the
way it all adds up, you ain't done shit. It all ends up small. It all
ends up sour.

BOSS OF BOSSES
by Joseph F. O'Brien and Andris Kurins
New York City - Present - Gloria Olarte (20's)

Gloria is the Godfather's housekeeper and mistress. Here she expresses some concern to a "sympathetic" FBI agent.

GLORIA: No, Meester Joe, I no theenk you understand. I no mean he keel heemself on purpose. I mean he do it by accident, weeth the needles.

[*The insulin?*]

[Sí. Yes.] Ees easy to make a bad meestake with the needle, and eef you make a bad meestake, you die.

[*But he's been injecting himself for years, said Joe O'Brien. Why would he make a mistake now?*]

He gets worse. Berry weak sometimes. Deezzy. And usually Gloria geeve him the insulin. Meester Paul's doctor, Dr. Hoffman, he show me how to do it. He say to me, 'Gloria, now remember thees, ees berry important. When you put the insulin een the syringe, always do like thees. Always make a leetle squirt come out. Because, remember, Gloria, eef there ees a leetle air, just a leetle bubble, eet gets into a vein, and goes around, and when eet hits the heart, she stops.' So I say, 'Hokay, Dr. Hoffman, I always be berry sure there ees no air.'

[*But if you do the needles—*]

But wait, Meester Joe. Thees ees what I'm telling you. The other morning, Gloria she ees downstairs, making the coffee for Meester Tommy. We wait for Meester Paul. And Meester Paul he no come down. We wait. And after a long time I get to worry. So I go upstairs. 'Meester Paul,' I call, 'Meester Paul. You come down now?' But there ees no answer.

So I go into his room, and Meester Paul he ees laying on the bed, but his legs are hanging off. His robe ees all twisted and his color ees all gray, like someone dead. His eyes roll back, only the white part ees showing. I run to him. 'Meester Paul, Meester Paul.' He say, 'Ah, Gloria, leetle Gloria.' He say eet berry strange, like groaning, like drunk. I say, 'Meester Paul, what ees wrong?' He say, berry soft, 'I don't know. I had my shot, I should feel better by now.' And then, on the bed, I see the syringe, and the syringe she ees dry. He must be berry deezzy, berry confuse, he forget to put in the insulin. He shoot in all air. If he hit a vein like that, already he is dead.

So now Gloria ees berry afraid. Fast like I can, I make a new needle, I shoot it in. But my hands shake. I cry. I berry afraid that Meester Paul die, that I lose Meester Paul. I say, 'Meester Paul, Meester Paul, you no take care of yourself anymore. Only Gloria she take care of you. Only Gloria take care.'

And Meester Paul, *gracias a Dios,* he come back berry fast. Once he have the insulin, he come back berry fast. He turn his head side to side, like he just wake up. And he say, 'Yes, Gloria, only you take care of me. No one else.' And I say, 'Promeese, Meester Paul. Promeese that you no geeve yourself the shots anymore, only Gloria geeve you the shots.' But he will not make thees promise. He says, 'No, thees I cannot say.' So now, ebery day, Gloria has to worry.

Paul, the Godfather, has been arrested and is in a car with two
FBI agents on the way to being indicted. He becomes talkative.

PAUL: Listen, [*he began,*] there's something I'd like you guys to
know. I don't know why I give a damn, but I do. I want you to
know I was never a womanizer. The occasional encounter, okay, it
happens. But I was never one to keep a mistress. I didn't need a
young babe at my elbow like a lotta these guys. I was too busy, I
didn't see the point. Besides—laugh if you want—I loved my wife.
And my kids. And it seemed to me, you cheat, you're not just
cheating on the woman, you're cheating on the whole family. That
didn't seem right to me.

All right, so now you say I'm an old fart, an old hypocrite, my
body's all messed up, I've got this young girlfriend, and I've been
a bastard to my poor dear wife. But it isn't quite that simple. I'm
old, yeah. I'm sick. But desire remains. Maybe it would be better
if it didn't, but it does. And what the hell is a man supposed to do
when desire remains and he simply cannot bring himself to touch his
wife ever again?

You guys are young. I'm sure your wives are pretty, and I hope
to God you enjoy each other. And I hope that what happened to me
never happens to you. It happened in the morning. That's when it
always happens, I think—never at night, but when you first crack an
eye, you wanna look at the new day and see some hope. You wake
up, you look over at your wife, who's still asleep. And you see an
old lady. Gray hair. Papery skin. Loose flesh. You're still fond
of her. In a way, maybe you even still love her. And you know
she's no older or more beat-up than you are. But you also know in
that moment you will never touch her again. You can't. Touching
her would be like making love with death.

CHICAGO LOOP
by Paul Theroux
Chicago - Present - Parker Jagoda (35-40)

Parker, although a family man, has developed an interest in
sado-masochism. Here, he tells a date from a singles ad he has
run, a story which he has made up as a test, for use at such
occasions.

PARKER: I was in a fraternity at Northwestern. Every Saturday
night a guy used to take a different girl there up the stairs and into
his room. We'd be watching from the kitchen. We didn't have
dates, and we were so envious of this guy. After about an hour, and
sometimes more, the girl would come out of the room, looking pale
and sort of dreamy and rumpled, and the guy behind her just staring
straight ahead to take her home. People get a certain look in their
eye after they've really had it—a kind of vacant, empty look, like
they've been punctured. Off they'd go. The following week it
would be someone else, the same look afterwards.

[*Some guys have the knack, Sharon said. But some chicks are
looking for it.*]

[*That's what we tried to find out, Parker said.*] So one Saturday
night we put a tape recorder under the bed in his room. Did I
mention he was Polish? But that's not important. He took a girl up.
They always looked so innocent. After an hour or so they left, and
she had that look but even more so, glittering from sex, and dazed,
because she'd had it over and over—her eyes were bright and
exhausted, like she had a fever.

[*What about the tape recorder?*]

As soon as they had gone we sneaked in and retrieved it, and we
took it into the attic to play the tape. It was really odd. There were
no voices on it at first. Then we heard the sound of sighs and grunts
and whispers. The girl was being held very hard—I imagined her
arm twisted behind her back, because I heard the guy say, 'Take off
your clothes and don't bother to scream, because if you do I'll snap
your arms in half, I'll pinch your head off'—and the girl whimpered

23

—'I'll cut your face so bad no one will look at you.' Then there were no more voices. The woman didn't say yes, she simply sighed harshly, like someone who's been burned, sort of surprise and shock, a sigh of dismay.

[*Maybe he tied her up, Sharon said hopefully.*]

[*Maybe very tight, Parker said.*] We heard the bed. We heard the struggle, and the breathing. It went on for a long time, and so did the silences. Then the gasps again, animal noises. After a long time we heard the door slam and it was over.

CHILDREN OF THE ARBAT
by Anatoli Rybakov
translated by Harold Shukman
Moscow - 1935 - Sofya (50's)

Sofya's brother Mark, a communist party functionary, has attempted to justify and explain away the arrest and exile to Siberia of her twenty-year-old son Sasha. Sofya replies.

SOFYA: Listen, Mark....First of all, while you're in my home never bang the table with your fist. I don't like it. Aside from my feelings, I have neighbors and it's embarrassing: my husband used to bang on the table, and now you're doing it. It must never happen again. Bang on your own table in your office, in front of your subordinates. Please don't forget this. As for the camps, don't threaten me—I'm not afraid of anything now, I've had enough of being afraid, and that's it. They can't put everyone inside, there aren't enough prisons....'A tiny minority.' How easy it is to say it! 'Millions of people are living in villages.' But have you seen how they live? Don't you remember, when you were young you used to sing 'Find me the village where the Russian peasant doesn't groan'? You sang it well, with heart, you were good, you pitied the peasant. Why don't you pity him anymore? Who were you singing about in those days? 'For the people, in the name of the people.' Isn't Sasha the people? Such an honest, openhearted boy, and so believing, and they send him to Siberia. They couldn't shoot him, so they send him to Siberia instead. What's left of your songs? Prisons, exile, camps. Now you pray to your Stalin....

[*Mark Alexandrovich stood up and pushed back his chair.*]

[*My dear sister—*]

Don't make a fuss, don't get excited, [*she continued calmly.*] Listen to what I have to say, Mark. You offered me money, but you can't buy yourself off. You've raised your sword against the innocent, against the defenseless, and you yourself will perish by the sword! [*She lowered her gray head and, looking at her brother from under her brows, she pointed a finger.*] And when your time comes, you'll remember Sasha, you'll think of him, but it'll be too late. You did not defend an innocent man. And there'll be nobody to defend you.

25

COLD SASSY TREE
by Olive Ann Burns
Georgia - 1906 - Grandpa Blakeslee (59)

Grandma is on her deathbed. Grandpa recollects sweet moments
to her through his pain.

GRANDPA: Here.

[*She tried to take the blossom but it fell to the sheet. Picking it
up, he sat staring at it, then spoke real low to her.*] I remember you
had a red rose like this'n in yore hair the day I decided to marry
you. Recollect thet Sunday, Miss Mattie Lou?

[*She kind of nodded and just barely smiled, her mouth listing to
the left.*]

I hadn't laid eyes on you since you was a li'l girl, till thet day.
You was sech a sweet thang, [*he said softly, his face close to hers,
his hand caressing her cheek.*] Yore eyes was all feisty and yore
feet patted out the organ music whilst we talked. Was thet really the
first time you ever set outside with the young folks, Miss Mattie
Lou? [*There was a twinkle in his eyes, a slight teasing in his voice,
almost like he'd forgot how sick she was.*] Gosh a'mighty, girl, thet
rafter-rattlin' preacher give us plenty time to git acquainted thet day,
didn't he? And I was after you like a charged-up bull. You
recollect thet day, Miss Mattie Lou?

[*She struggled to speak, her voice a whisper. 'Member...the
brush arbor...Mr. Bla'slee?*]

[*As Grandpa held her hand tight and tears rolled down his
cheeks, I thought how Granny used to tell me about them camping
out under a thick brush arbor their whole first married summer while
Grandpa and Uncle Ephraim Toy built her a two-room house out of
poplar logs so big it took just five to make a wall.*]

[*I had figured out long time ago that my mother must have been
conceived under the brush arbor—and I blushed to think about that
now. Whether such memories were stirring in Grandpa, who can
know. What he said next was*] Miss Mattie Lou, try real hard and
git well. You hear? Please git well. I don't want to live 'thout
you.

COLD SASSY TREE
by Olive Ann Burns
Georgia - 1906 - Grandpa Blakeslee (59)

Grandma is dying. Grandpa talks to God in his very personal style.

GRANDPA: Lord? [*he began, then stopped to honk his nose into a handkerchief.*] Lord, I'm tempted to ast You to make Miss Mattie Lou well, like You was one a-them Atlanta doctors, or maybe Santy Claus and her a Christmas present You could give me if'n You jest would. I know Thou don't mind me hopin' she'll git well, Lord, or wishin', but hep me not to beg You to spare her....Oh God, You know my sin! [*he cried suddenly. His voice had an awful sound, like he was about to break half in two.*]

[*What could be his sin?*]

[*Granny's harsh breathing and the hushed voices in the parlor filled the silence. Finally he went on.*] If'n she lives, Lord, I'll be thet thankful. If'n she don't pull th'ew, I ain't go'n say it was Thy will. You wouldn't kill her, Lord, to punish me....Hep me remember my faith that Yore arrangement for livin' and dyin' is good. Hit ain't fair or equal, Lord, but it keeps thangs movin' on. Hep me not forgit my faith thet whatever happens, it's all right.... Hep Will Tweedy here see thet we got to accept dyin' in exchange for livin' and workin', and havin' folks like Miss Mattie Lou to love. And be loved by.

[*My grandfather's voice was stronger and calmer now.*] Lord, [*he added, like it was a postscript on a letter,*] please forgive the ways I ain't done right by Miss Mattie Lou. Please, forgive me. She don't know, and ain't nobody else knows, but I know and You know, Lord, what I'm a-talkin' bout. And please hep her stand the sufferin'. Hep her not be skeered. And wilt thou please comfort them grievin' daughters in the parlor, Lord, and Will Tweedy here, and li'l Mary Toy. Give them heart's ease. And me, too, Lord. A-men.

COLD SASSY TREE
by Olive Ann Burns
Georgia - 1906 - Grandpa Blakeslee (59)

Grandpa has just eloped with his bookkeeper, Miss Love, three
weeks after his wife of forty-odd years died. He comforts his
children and grandchildren after dinner. All is tense until his
goodbye.

GRANDPA: Well, folks, [*said Grandpa, taking aholt of her
elbow,*] I reckon we best mosey on home now. Hit's been a long
fancy day.
  [*Miss Love looked at me. How are you feeling now, Will?*]
  [*Pretty good, ma'am.*]
  Fore we go, [*said Grandpa,*] I'd like all y'all to join me and
my wife in a word a-prayer.
  [*You can't hardly refuse a man that.*]
  [*In stony silence they all bowed their heads, where they stood or
sat. With his right arm around Miss Love and his left arm stub laid
across my shoulder and me facing the two of them, Grandpa
prayed.*]
  [*I didn't close my eyes. I was too busy watching faces—Mama's
and Papa's and Aunt Loma's and, of course, Miss Love's. Clasping
her hands together, she closed those gray-blue eyes and ducked her
head down and all I could see then was the big mass of wavy brown
hair and the little blue hat. I noticed for the first time that her hair
had a lot of gray sprinkled through it.*]
  [*After what Grandpa had been saying to me in the kitchen, I
should of been prepared for what he said to God in the parlor:*]
Lord above, afore this gatherin' assembled, I ast You to bless the
memory of Miss Mattie Lou.
  [*Everybody gasped. Nobody expected him to bring her up.*]
  [*Grandpa didn't seem to hear the gasps.*] Please God, forgive
me all the ways I ain't done right by her. Thou knowest what she
meant to me and our chi'ren, Mary Willis and Loma, [*he continued,*]
and to Will Tweedy and li'l Mary Toy. [*There was a pause, his*]

28

face working like he might not could go on, but he did.] And now I ast yore blessin' on this here girl I married today. [*Miss Love raised her head and stared up at Grandpa, mouth agape. I do think his were the only eyes in the room still shut.*] Lord, hep me be good to her. You know I need Miss Love. Hep her to need me likewise. And give her the grace to unner-stand thet if'n they's aught to respect in me, it's because a-thet one in the grave out yonder, what all she learnt me.

THE DEATH OF METHUSELAH AND OTHER STORIES
A Peephole in the Gate
by Isaac Beshevis Singer
Atlantic Ocean - 1920-40 - Sam (60's)

Sam explains his distrust of women by recollecting a shipboard
experience which occurred as he was fleeing from his unfaithful
wife.

SAM: After what happened with Eve I trusted no one. Among us
greenhorns there was a little young woman who was returning to
America. She had gone back to Europe to bring over her aunt.
They both occupied a cabin, but the old woman became seasick, so
the niece spent most of her time with us, the immigrants. Her
husband was a ritual slaughterer in Brownsville. What did we know
about Brownsville? In Warsaw the wife of a ritual slaughterer wore
a wig or a bonnet, but this woman went about with her head
uncovered. She was dark, with laughing eyes. She pulled jokes out
of her sleeve. Every day I gave her a large slice of salami. She
nicknamed me Baby, even though I was tall and she so tiny I could
have put her in my pocket. She was a big talker and clever as the
dickens. For her, things didn't have to be spelled out. One look
and she knew all about you, like a gypsy. Her name was Becky.
Though her real name was Breindel, in America it became Becky.
I never met anyone so quickly. She was everywhere and knew
everything. She hopped around like a bird. Of course she could
speak English. She said to me, 'Baby dear, if one woman was false
to you, it isn't necessary to blame all of us.' 'How do you know
that a woman was false to me?' I asked. 'Baby, it's written on your
forehead,' she answered. The next day Becky invited me to her
cabin. Her aunt lay there as if she were dead. Seasickness is a
terrible thing. I thought that she was dying, but Becky was laughing
and winking at me. She signaled me to lean toward her while she
raised herself on her tiptoes. She gave me a kiss that I still
remember. That the wife of a ritual slaughterer should kiss a strange
man was something new to me. I said to her, 'Don't you love your

30

husband?' and she replied, 'Yes, I do love him, but he's busy slaughtering in Brownsville and I'm here.' 'If he knew what you were doing he would slaughter you, too.' And she said, 'If people knew the truth, the world would collapse like a house of cards.' We made love right then and there. I never knew that such a small woman could have such large desires. She tired me out, not I her. All the while she kept on prattling about God. Sabbath Eve she put three candles into three potatoes, draped a shawl over her head, covered her eyes with her fingers, and blessed the candles. And so we arrived in America. On the dock a large crowd stood waiting for the new arrivals, and my piece of merchandise recognized her husband, the slaughterer. 'Listen, Baby,' she said to me, 'nothing happened between us. We are complete strangers, forget the whole thing.' I later saw her hugging the slaughterer. She kissed him and wept, and I renewed my oath never to believe a woman. Shloimele, I said to myself, it's a false world. Years later a rabbi told me that it's written in the Torah that all humans are liars.

DO OR DIE
by Léon Bing
An LA reform school - Present - G-Roc (15)

G-Roc, an incarcerated Crips gang member, eschews rape and tells why.

G-ROC: I mean, my homeboys be doin' rapes, but I'm like, 'Man, y'all go on with that ol' type shit, man—I ain't doin' no rape.' They, you know, they'll just rape a girl, any girl, if she look good and she don't wanna kick in. [*Now he turns to face me again.*] Hey, if they want it bad enough, they gonna take it. All of them together. And beat on her, too, if she try to hold back. That's why I don't do all that, you know, because I wouldn't want nobody raping *my* girl, or my mama, you know? Man, I'd fuck around and be on Death Row if somebody did me like that. You know, on the outs this pig was sayin', 'You shouldn't steal because then somebody steal from you.' And I agree with that, but the kinda stealin' I'm sayin', well… [*He begins to stammer in his earnestness to get his thought across. His voice doesn't sound so much like a man's now, it is merely the husky rasp of a teenager.*] It's like, like…I steal, but I don't jack. Like, people jack, like… [*He begins to act is out now, his voice plummeting into his chest,*] 'Get out yo' car!' [*His voice returns to normal.*] You know? I jack that way but I don't jack like— [*back to the low scary tones again—*] 'Give up yo' wallet!' and all like that, 'cause I got money. I don't have to pull a gun on nobody for they money. [*Tiny Vamp nods vigorously, sensing a way back into G-Roc's better graces.*] And jewelry. [*He pronounces it like the word "jury."*] I won't jack nobody for no jewelry—or drugs—or money. Car. I'll jack for a car.

Ye-eeeeeh. [*G-Roc draws the word out of his mouth as if it were a long strand of bubble gum.*] I'll jack for a car. I *got* a car, though—big old Monte Carlo. Had an Essay fix it up for me, all white with blue pearl and chrome-base gold leaf. Look *good.* So if I jack for a car it's only for somethin' we can use for like shootings, or g-rides, you know? But, like I said, I wouldn't jack nobody for they money. All that ain't called for. I *got* money— [*he hisses loudly again—*] I sell dope for *my* money.

32

DO OR DIE
by Léon Bing
Los Angeles - Present - Faro (17)

Faro, a homeless gang member, explains the "rules of engagement."

FARO: I watch out for the little kids in my neighborhood. So gangs who we don't get along with [—*he names several sets, both Bloods and Crips—*] don't come in and shoot 'em up. All them I just named, they come in and shoot us up, then we catch one of 'em slippin' and it's all over for them.

[*He is looking at the children as he talks. His voice is soft, but somehow it is now calm.*]

Like there was this fool, this enemy nigger from our worst enemy set, and he was with his wife and his baby. They was walkin' down there near Vermont, where he had no business bein'. He was slippin' bad and we caught him. We was in a car, all homies, and I was like, 'Let's pop this dumb nigger, let's empty the whole clip in him.' [*Faro turns to look at me, as if he wants to make sure I understand what he is saying.*] We had an AK— two-barrel banana clips, two sides—and I just... [*He hesitates only for an instant.*] I just wanted to make him pay.

[*Careful to keep my voice as soft as his, I ask him what it was he wanted the guy to pay for.*]

For all our dead homeboys. For bein' our enemy. For slippin' so bad. [*He is warming to his subject, his voice is coming alive now.*] You gotta understand—enemy got to pay just for bein' alive. [*He is quiet for a moment, then he gives a little hitch of his shoulders, like a prizefighter, and he goes on. He is animated now, reliving the event for me.*] I was like 'fuck it, Cuz—I'm gonna strap this shit to the seat and I'm just gonna *work* it. [*He twists around to face the passenger door and mimes the action of holding and aiming an AK-47 rifle.*] So I strapped it to the seat, like this, and we circled around and pulled up on this nigger from two blocks away, crept up on him slow like, and I just gave it to him. [*Faro begins

33

to jerk and buck there in his seat as the imaginary weapon in his hands fires automatically.] *Pah-pah-pah-pah-pah-pah-pah!* You know, just let him have it. Just emptied the whole... [*He is wholly caught up in his recollection, inflamed with it, drunk with it.*] I lit his ass *up!* I killed him—shot his baby in the leg—crippled his wife! [*He is facing me again, his eyes fixed on some point just to the left of mine.*] She in a wheelchair now, I heard, wearin' a voicebox, 'cause one of the bullets caught her in the throat. [*Then, in afterthought,*] The baby okay.

DO OR DIE
by Léon Bing
Los Angeles - Present - Faro (17)

Faro, a homeless gang member, talks of life and death.

FARO: That's a crazy world out there, and we livin' in it.

[*Dying in it, too.*]

[*The finger stops tapping.*]

If you die, you die. Most gangbangers don't have nothin' to live for no more, anyway. That why some of 'em be gangbangin'.

[*He seems to sense what it is that I'm thinking.*]

I ain't just talkin' 'bout myself, either. I'm talkin' for a lotta gangbangers. They mothers smokin' dope. Or somebody shot somebody else's mother, and that person figure if they gangbang they got a chance to get 'em back. People don't have nothin' to live for if they mother dead, they brother dead, they sister dead. What else they got to live for? If people in yo' family is just dyin', if the person you love the most, the person who love *you* the most be dead, then what else *do* you got to live for?

[*Yourself.*]

[*It's as if I hadn't spoken; he doesn't even hear me.*]

I tell you this—you see enough dyin', then you be ready to die yourself, just so you don't have to see no more of death.

DONNIE BRASCO: MY UNDERCOVER LIFE IN THE MAFIA
by Joseph D. Pistone with Richard Woodley
New York City - 1970's - Lefty (30-40)

FBI agent Joseph F. Pistone has infiltrated the mob using the alias Donnie Brasco. Here Lefty, Donnie's mentor, lectures Donnie regarding the proper attitude for a contract hit.

LEFTY: No, Donnie, you don't understand. It ain't that simple. That's why I gotta school you. Hitting a guy on a contract is a lot different than whacking a guy over a beef. On a beef, you got a rage about the guy. But on a contract you might have no feelings one way or another about the guy, it might not even concern you why the guy's getting hit. You got to be able to do it just like a professional job, with no emotion at all. [*You think you could do that?*]

[*I don't see why not.*]

[*Yeah, well, we'll see.*] Lot of guys think it's easy, then they freeze up and can't do it. Next time I get a contract, I'll take you with me, show you how to do it. Generally you use a .22. A .22 doesn't make a clean hole like some bigger calibers. Just right behind the ear. A .22 ricochets around your skull, tears everything up. Next contract I get, I'll take you along.

THE FEVER
by Wallace Shawn
Dictatorship - Present - Man - Any age

Traveling in a poor country, a man confronts himself.

MAN: Don't you think—when you're traveling in a strange country—that the smells are sharp and upsetting? And when you wake up in the middle of the night—unexpectedly—when you wake up at an odd hour—when you're traveling somewhere and you wake up in a strange place—don't you feel frightened?

I can't stop shivering.

The lamp by my bed doesn't work, the electric lights won't turn on. The rebels have blown up the electricity towers. There's a small war going on in this poor country where my language isn't spoken. The hotel rooms all have candles with little candle holders. I get up, light the candle, take the candle into the bathroom. Then I put the candle in its holder on the floor, and I kneel down in front of the toilet and vomit.—Then I'm sitting, shivering, on the bathroom floor, this cold square of tile on a hot night in a hot country, and I can't stand up to go back to bed—I can't stand up—so I sit there quietly, shaking as if I were sitting in the snow. And in the corner of the bathroom—brown against the tile—there's an insect, big, like a water bug—it's flat, heavy—very tough legs, they look like metal—and it's waiting, squatting, deciding which way to move. —And in a second it's crossed behind the sink, and it's slipping itself into a hole too small for it to fit in, but it fits—in—it fits—it's gone. And I see myself. I see myself. A moment of insight.

GORKY PARK
by Martin Cruz Smith
Moscow - Present - Irina Asanova (20's)

Irina and her lover Arkady are caught between two bad choices.
She has spent many years in Siberia and tells him this story.

IRINA: You know what the 'Siberian dilemma' is?
  [*No.*]
It's a choice between two ways of freezing. We were out on a
lake fishing through the ice when a teacher of ours fell through. He
didn't go far, just down to his neck, but we knew what was
happening. If he stayed in the water he would freeze to death in
thirty or forty seconds. If he got out he would freeze to death at
once—he would be ice, actually. He taught gymnastics, I remember.
He was an Evenki, the only native on the teaching staff, young,
everyone liked him. We all stood about in a circle around the hole
holding our poles and fish. It was about minus forty degrees, bright
and sunny. He had a wife, a dentist; she wasn't along. He looked
up at us; I'll never forget that look. He couldn't have been in the
water for more than five seconds when he pulled himself out.
  [*And?*]
He was dead before he stood up. But he got out, that was the
important thing. He didn't just wait to die.

GORKY PARK
by Martin Cruz Smith
Moscow - Present - Arkady Renko (30's)

Police investigator Renko has discovered that his lover is also
the lover of the man he is tracking. He confronts her with his
knowledge.

ARKADY: You slept with Osborne in Moscow. You sleep with
him here. He showed me the bed. I want you to tell me about it.
You did intend to tell me about it sometime, didn't you?
  [*Arkasha, she said so softly that he could hardly hear what she
had said.*]
  One man is not enough for you? [*Arkady asked.*] Or Osborne
does something for you that I don't? Something special, a particular
position? Backward, forward? Please inform me. Or he possesses
a sexual magnetism you can't resist? Are you attracted to a man
whose hands are covered with blood? See, my hands are blood now.
Not the blood of *your* friends, I'm afraid—only the blood of *my*
friend.
  [*He held his bloody hands up for her to see.*] No [*—he read her
reaction—*] not satisfactory, not stimulating enough. But Osborne
tried to kill you; maybe that's the difference. That's it!

THE HOUSE OF THE SPIRITS
by Isabel Allende
South America - 1900 - Nivea (50's)

Here, Nivea tells her daughter Clara a story about a tree linked
to both tradition and misfortune in the del Valle family.

NIVEA: It was an enormous tree, [*she would say.*] I had it cut
before my oldest son was born. They say it was so tall that you
could see the whole city from its top, but the only one who got that
high had no eyes to see it with. It was a tradition in the del Valle
family that when any of the young men wanted to wear long pants,
he had to climb it to prove his valor. It was like an initiation rite.
The tree was full of marks. I saw them with my own eyes when
they knocked it down. From the first middle-sized branches, which
were thick as chimneys, you could already see the marks left by the
grandfathers, who had made the same ascent in their own youth.
From the initials cut into the trunk you could tell who had climbed
higher, who was the bravest, as well as who had stopped, too
terrified to continue. One day it was the turn of Jerónimo, the blind
cousin. He began the climb feeling his way up the branches without
a moment's hesitation, for he couldn't see how high up he was and
had no intuition of the void. He reached the top, but he wasn't able
to complete the J of his initial, because he came unstuck like a
gargoyle and plummeted headfirst to the ground, landing at the feet
of his father and brothers. He was fifteen years old. They wrapped
the body in a sheet and took it to his mother, who spat in all their
faces and shouted at them with a sailor's insults and cursed the men
who had induced her son to climb the tree, until finally the Sisters
of Charity came to cart her off in a straitjacket. I knew that one day
my sons would be expected to continue the barbarous tradition.
That's why I had them cut it down. I didn't want Luis and the other
children growing up in the shadow of that scaffold in the courtyard.

THE HOUSE OF THE SPIRITS
by Isabel Allende
South America - 1900 - Nivea (50's)

The mother of Clara and Rosa tells Clara a cautionary tale about
the girl's Uncle Juan, who was the victim of an accident that had
tragic consequences.

NIVEA: And this, [*she would say,*] is your Uncle Juan. I loved
him very much. He once farted and that became his death sentence:
a great disgrace. It was during a picnic lunch. All my cousins and
I were out together on the most fragrant spring afternoon, with our
muslin dresses and our hats full of flowers and ribbons, and the boys
were wearing the Sunday best. Juan took off his white jacket—why,
I can see him now! He rolled up his sleeves and swung gracefully
from the branch of a tree, hoping that with his trapeze artist's skill
he could win the admiration of Constanza Andrade, the Harvest
Queen, with whom, from the moment he laid eyes on her, he had
been desperately in love. Juan did two impeccable push-ups and one
complete somersault, but on his next flip over he let go a loud burst
of wind. Don't laugh, Clara! It was terrible. There was an
embarrassed silence and the Harvest Queen began to laugh
uncontrollably. Juan put on his jacket and grew very pale. He
walked slowly away from the group and we never saw him again.
They even looked for him in the Foreign Legion. They asked for
him in all the consulates, but he was never heard of again. I think
he must have become a missionary and gone to minister to the lepers
out on Easter Island, which is as far away as a man can go to forget
and be forgotten because it's not on the normal routes of navigation
and isn't even shown on Dutch maps. From that day on, he was
referred to as Juan of the Fart.

THE HOUSE OF THE SPIRITS
by Isabel Allende
South America - 1900 - Esteban Trueba (30's)

Esteban is a tall, imperious man with a regal demeanor, striking
visage, powerful stride and an explosive temper. Following the
death of his fiance Rosa, Esteban comes to reclaim an
abandoned house occupied years ago by his family. He decries
the selfishness of the peasants living in the town surrounding his
hacienda.

ESTEBAN: Unfortunately, the only thing that really works in these
countries is the stick. This isn't Europe. What you need here is a
strong government, with a strong man. It would be lovely if we
were all created equal, but the fact is we're not. It couldn't be more
obvious. The only one who knows how to work around here is me,
and I defy you to prove otherwise. I'm the first one up and the last
one to bed in this godforsaken place. If it were up to me, I'd send
it all packing and go live like a prince in the capital, but I have to
stay here, because if I were to leave for so much as a week, it would
all collapse and these poor creatures would be starving to death again
before you know it. Just remember what it was like when I arrived
here years ago: a wasteland. It was a ruin filled with rocks and
vultures. A no-man's-land. All the pastures were overgrown. No
one had thought of channeling the water. They were satisfied to
plant their dirty little lettuce plants in their front yards and let the
rest of it sink into misery. I had to come in order for there to be
law and order here, and work. How could I be anything but proud?
I've worked so well that I've already bought up the two neighboring
haciendas. This property is now the biggest and richest in the whole
area—an example, the envy of everyone around, a model hacienda.
And with the new highway going right alongside us its value has
doubled. It I wanted to sell out, I could go the Europe and live off
the interest, but I'm not going anywhere. This is where I plan to
stay, killing myself. I'm doing it for them. If it weren't for me,
they'd be lost. If we go to the heart of the matter, they're useless

42

even for running errands. As I've always said, they're like children. There's not one of them can do what he's supposed to do without me there behind him driving him on. And then they start in on me with the story that we are all equal! It's enough to make you die laughing!

THE IMPOSTER
by Paula Sharp
New York City - Present - Mrs. Dupont (50's)

Mrs. Dupont hitches a ride in a limousine in New York's financial district. She says she is on the way home from the hospital and then reveals some very personal matters to the male passenger, Byron Coffin.

MRS. DUPONT: I know in my heart of hearts that Russell—my brother—will recover too! They're going to blast that tumor with chemotherapy and they say it could all but vanish in only three sessions. Then they do thirteen more just to make sure it doesn't dare rear its ugly head again. They're horrifying it back to wherever it came from. He just happens to be in excruciating pain in the meantime.

[Byron knew what would happen next, and it did: an outburst.]

[Mrs. Dupont turned to Antoinette.] It's not my brother! [she wailed. Byron thought he had misunderstood her, but the Mrs. Dupont said,] It's another man! I've been seeing him six months. [She made an effort at self-restraint, wiping her eyes and sitting up straight.] Don't get me wrong, [she said, placing her hand yet again on Byron's arm.] I was faithful to my husband for twenty years and I expected to be for twenty more. Then, all of a sudden, there I was in love with a man I met on the PATH train! We're head over heels! I lead a double life now, like Mr. Jekyll and Mr. Hyde. I'm ordinarily a very sane, sensible woman, Mr. Coffin.

[Doctor.]

[What?]

[Of course you meant Dr. Jekyll and Mr. Hyde, Byron corrected her, but he noted an unintended consoling tone in his voice. Mrs. Dupont seemed satisfied.]

And the terrible thing is, I can't even visit him in his hospital room, because his wife would know. I sit in the waiting area for hours and hours just hoping for a member of his family to walk by discussing him. I hear them in his room, talking in low voices to

44

each other. I feel like a criminal, having to hide like that! Imagine not being able to be with your loved one at such a time, because what binds you is a secret, and if you break the secret, you'll be torn asunder.

THE IMPOSTER
by Paula Sharp
Wisconsin - Present - Daisy (38)

Daisy has just been jilted for a younger, prettier woman. She
tells a friend how she feels about it.

DAISY: Oh Netta, he's such a big beautiful illusion of a man!
[*Daisy Shedailo warned me. She leaned forward on my mother's
couch, balancing an empty can of Blatz beer on the armrest.*] I used
to think he treated me nice. But when he dragged me to this
Wisconsin hellhole, everything changed. Whenever I told him I
didn't want to mind his boys, he'd say, 'That's really beneath you,
Day, I can't believe you talking about two little kids that way, Day,'
and I'd say, 'I just want a little time alone with you, just to pretend
that I'm at the center of somebody's world the way you're at the
center of mine.' It took me so long to realize he just wanted his
own free at no cost slave babysitter. [*Daisy creased the Blatz can
and bent it double.*] I feel sorry for that girl, whoever she is!

When I met him, I thought he was so wonderful, such a
responsible father to his kids—*responsible* isn't the word, he didn't
have a penny in his pocket for us after he paid his wife maintenance.
And those goddamn pigs! I thought I'd lose my mind watching
them, I'd find myself thinking, God if they'd just wander on the road
and get hit by cars, so we could pack up and move to the city and
get out of god-awful Ripon.

[*She settled the beer can on the floor and looked at me
defiantly.*] I swear I'd kill that girl if I knew who she was! Who is
she to weasel in on us so soon after we separated? Christ, these
local girls don't learn jackshit about contraception, how do I know
she isn't pregnant?

I want him back! All I feel is this terrible loss, this emptiness,
right here, over my thighs, right smack in the center of me, this
emptiness that goes on and on, big as life. Don't ever do what I
did! Don't ever promise not to have children just for some man!
Because you know what I want now more than anything is real
children, my children. I want one named Sherry and another one
who's tall like my father. And I'm never going to have any of that!
How am I supposed to start over at the age of thirty-eight?

INTERVIEWING MATISSE or
THE WOMAN WHO DIED STANDING UP
by Lily Tuck
Connecticut - Present - Molly (30-50)

Molly telephones Lily after midnight to tell her that their friend
Inez has just been found dead. They talk for hours. Here,
Molly dissects Inez's live-in lover Kevin.

MOLLY: And did I tell you what else Price said? Claude-Marie
said Price said he could tell by just looking at Kevin what kind of
bartender Kevin was. I know what Price means, Lily. I could tell,
too, by how Kevin lounged around all day on the couch—the same
couch Inez wanted to throw out—and how Kevin wore nothing but
a pair of old running shorts and Kevin did not run. No. Price ran.
Price ran a marathon once, remember? Kevin used to just sit there
and ask Inez to bring him stuff—his cigarettes, his beer, her ass
once. Poor Inez. And Inez said she was allergic to smoke, to
cigarette smoke, and I remember the time Inez's mother was
smoking a—oh, have you met Inez's mother, Lily? You met her at
the birthday party, and Inez's mother is not at all the way I pictured
Inez's mother to be or the way Inez was. No, no. Inez's mother is
blond, Inez's mother is remarried, Inez's mother chain smokes, and
the time I am telling you about now, Lily, Inez kept getting up from
where she was sitting and opening up the window and this was in
winter and this was after Price had left—after Price and Inez had
separated already, but before Price had remarried yet—and Inez kept
telling her mother how she was going to ruin and kill off the
gardenia plants with her cigarette smoke and Inez's mother kept
telling Inez how Inez was going to kill *her* off with pneumonia if she
did not sit down right this minute and shut the window. Hello?

INTERVIEWING MATISSE or
THE WOMAN WHO DIED STANDING UP
by Lily Tuck
Connecticut - Present - Molly (30-50)

Molly telephones Lily after midnight to tell her that their friend
Inez has just been found dead. They talk for hours. Here,
Molly discusses Inez's mother and her love for the telephone.

MOLLY: Yes, but one thing, though—the thing Inez and her
mother had in common—they both liked to talk on the phone a lot.
I'll never forget this, Lily, and this was what Inez told me and,
swear to God, this is true and what Inez said to me. Inez said, that
when she, Inez, was little, her father had tried to call, call home
from his office, and the phone was busy all morning. So, Inez's
father got into his car and he drove all the way back home—this was
still in Wisconsin—and without a single word to Inez's mother, who
was still talking on the phone, Inez's father yanked the phone, wire
and all, right out of the wall. He left a big hole there, and he never
once said a word to Inez's mother, and what Inez said was that as
long as she lived, she, Inez, would never forget the hole in the wall
where the phone was.

INTERVIEWING MATISSE or
THE WOMAN WHO DIED STANDING UP
by Lily Tuck
Connecticut - Present - Molly (30-50)

Molly telephones Lily after midnight to tell her that their friend
Inez has just been found dead. They talk for hours. Here,
Molly reminisces about her hometown.

MOLLY: Strange, too, what this makes me think of. This makes
me think of my own father. My own father did not wear bow ties,
Lily and my father did not die of a heart attack. My father died of
an aneurism sitting right there at his desk, and what this makes me
think of is how my father said he wanted to be cremated. Cremated
in his white linen suit, he said. A suit he had had made to measure
in England—especially. Only when he died, the suit no longer fit
him. My mother had to have the white linen suit altered, Lily. I
tried to talk my mother out of it—out of letting out the suit. I told
my mother if my father was going to be buried this would have been
different. My mother said I was hard-hearted and, what was more,
I had no respect for the dead. I said to her: After all, I am just
trying to be practical, and when I told Claude-Marie—told Claude-
Marie what my mother had said—Claude-Marie said he knew all
along anyway that all Southerners were crazy. Virginians.
Virginians is what I keep reminding Claude-Marie, and I keep telling
Claude-Marie there is a big difference. Virginians, I tell Claude-
Marie, are not Southerners. Virginians are different. I had the
same discussion with Yuri once. Yuri is Russian, and Russians, too,
are different. In a way, Lily, Russians are a lot like Virginians. I
told Yuri, he, Yuri, would have loved my mother. Only you cannot
believe everything Yuri says—for instance, about his own mother.
Yuri is always saying how his mother knew Chekhov, and Chekhov,
we all know, died in 1904, which would mean that Yuri's mother
was over a hundred years old—oh, like Havier's grandmother. You
know my friend Havier in Old Saybrook—Havier who helped me
with the seagull, Havier who is Fred's lover? According to Havier,

INTERVIEWING MATISSE or
THE WOMAN WHO DIED STANDING UP

his grandmother has nineteen children, sixty-four grandchildren, and God knows how many great grandchildren, and Havier, because he is gay, is the only one in his family, he says, except for one sister, who has something wrong with her ovaries, not to have any children. Inez—when I told her this—Inez could not believe this. Inez only has the one sister—Patricia. And Patricia has no children. Patricia, Inez said, had electroshock treatment. Patricia moved to Hawaii. Lily? Electroshock treatment, Lily, is not as bad as it sounds and a lot of people I know have had it. Amy, my best friend from school in Charlottesville, has. Amy had electroshock treatment because she saw monkeys—monkeys instead of people. Oh, did I say Charlottesville, Lily? I said Charlottesville because Charlottesville is simpler. I lived in a small town outside of Charlottesville. But Crozet is not really a small town either. Crozet is a bunch of houses, a general store, a post office. What's more, no one has ever heard of Crozet, and if Claude-Marie thinks all Southerners are crazy, Claude-Marie should have lived in Crozet.

KISS OUT
by Jill Eisenstadt
Queens, New York - Present - Fred (26)

The family is gathered at the Passover table. Mom wants the
whole ceremony. Dad wants to paraphrase it for the assembled.
Fred does instead.

FRED: The Jews, [*Fred begins,*] were slaves in Egypt. Because
the pharaoh was a real dick...tator. He rarely fed them. Always
whipped them. Had them chained up by the ankles and wrists. The
living conditions were intensely foul and unlivable. Basically, the
brute broke their balls in every—
    [*Fred!, Mom says.*]
    [*Alliteration, Oscar allows.*]
    —every way his limited imagination could dream up. And the
Jews, forced to lug around marble and build pyramids or sewage
systems, whatever, roads, had a lot of time to gripe to God about
this hor-rendous state of affairs, which they did regularly to no avail
until da dada daaa! *Moses shows.* [*Fred imagines, not the
Claymation version, but the real Hollywood thing, Charlton Heston.*]
A very charismatic guy who knows how to loosen God up some, get
him chatting. [*After Charlton has his rendezvous with the Almighty,
he returns with this bushy beard and big gray pompadour.*] And,
OK, God's kind of a tightwad—
    [*Fred!, Mom says.*]
    —about divulging his name. Well, he was! But he did come out
with that classic line that Popeye would steal centuries later, '*I am
what I am.*' And he came through in the clutch with the plagues.
My fave. Too bad the movie only skims it. But anyway, fun ahead,
you all get to dribble wine on the tablecloth as a lesson not to go
partying over other people's misfortunes. *Ready,* are you? *Set...?*
    [*Go!, Louette finishes, rejuvenated by the idea of some
vandalism. She still carries a gold metallic marker around
everywhere in her purse.*]
    Blood! Frogs! Vermin! Flies! Locusts! [*Fred's voice cracks*

51

with a genuine thrill.] *Murrain!* [*Oscar tries to interrupt to tell how the frogs are always escaping in the PetMart, but interruption will not be tolerated just now.*] *Boils! Hail!* [*Hersh slings his wine around, dousing the tablecloth.*] *Locusts! Darkness!* And *the slaying of the firstborn!*

[*Some nice God, murmurs Mary.*]

[*Big shot, says Louette.*]

And these nasty displays of what I'd have to call divine machismo got us outta there. Along with the Red Sea episode, which scientists say could have been a tidal phenomenon. [*Silence. So Fred tacks on,*] The end. [*They all continue to look at him. After what seems a long while, he breaks down and asks,*] Well, elders? [*for approval, applause, coins.*] Did I get it right or what?

LIFE AND FATE
by Vasily Grossman
translated from Russian by Robert Chandler
Russia - 1939-1940 - Mrs. Shtrum (60)

Mrs. Shtrum, a Russian doctor who has been trapped in her
small village by the German invasion, writes to her son in
Moscow about the atrocities which have begun and the ominous
implications for the future. Here she concludes with a farewell.

MRS. SHTRUM: Vityenka, I'm finishing this letter and taking it to
the ghetto fence to hand to my friend. It's not easy to break off.
It's my last conversation with you. Once I send it off, I will have
left you for ever and you will never know of my last hours. This is
our final parting. What can I say to you in farewell, in eternal
farewell? These last days, as during my whole life, you have been
my joy. I've remembered you at night, the clothes you wore as a
boy, your first books. I've remembered your first letter, your first
day at school. I've remembered everything, everything from the
first days of your life to the last news that I heard from you, the
telegram I received on the 30th of June. I've closed my eyes and
imagined that you were shielding me, my dearest, from the horror
that is approaching. And then I've remembered what is happening
here and felt glad that you were apart from me—and that this terrible
fate will pass you by!

Vitya, I've always been lonely. I've wept in anguish through
lonely nights. My consolation was the thought of how I would tell
you one day about my life. Tell you why your father and I
separated, why I have lived on my own for so many years. And
I've often thought how surprised my Vitya would be to learn how his
mother made mistakes, raved, grew jealous, made others jealous,
was just what young people always are. But my fate is to end my
life alone, never having shared it with you. Sometimes I've thought
that I ought not to live far away from you, that I love you too much,
that love gives me the right to be with you in my old age. And at
other times I've thought that I ought not to live together with you,

53

that I love you too much.

Well, *enfin*...Always be happy with those you love, those around you, those who have become closer to you than your mother. Forgive me.

I can hear women weeping on the street, and policemen swearing; as I look at these pages, they seem to protect me from a terrible world that is filled with suffering.

How can I finish this letter? Where can I find the strength, my son? Are there words capable of expressing my love for you? I kiss you, your eyes, your forehead, your hair.

Remember that your mother's love is always with you, in grief and in happiness, no one has the strength to destroy it.

Vityenka...This is the last line of your mother's last letter to you. Live, live, live for ever...Mama.

LILA
by Robert M. Pirsig
New York City - Present - Lila (30's)

Phaedrus has picked up Lila during a drunken evening and they have slept together. Now he is trying to find out what she's all about. She resists his interrogation.

LILA: You know something?
   [*What?*]
   You're not drinking as much as I am. [*She held the bottle up to the sky and looked at it.*] And you know something else?
   [*What?*]
   I'm not going to answer any more of your questions.
   [*Why not?*]
   You're the detective. That's what you are. You think you're going to learn something, I don't know what, but you're not going to learn anything....You'll never find out who I am because I'm not anything.
   [*What do you mean?*]
   I'm not anybody. All these questions you're asking are just a waste of time. I know you're trying to find out what kind of a person I am but you're never going to find out anything because there's nothing to know.
   [*Her voice was getting slushy. She could tell it was getting slushy.*]
   I mean, I used to play I was this kind of person and that kind of person but I got so tired of playing all those games. It's such work and it doesn't do any good. There's just all these pictures of who I am and they don't hold together. They're all different people I'm supposed to be but none of them are me. I'm not anybody. I'm not here. Like you now. I can see you've got a lot of bad impressions about me in your mind. And you think that what's in your mind is here talking to you but nobody's here. You know what I mean? Nobody's home. That's Lila. Nobody's home.
   You know what? [*Lila said.*]

55

LILA

[*What?*]

What you want to do is make me into something I'm not.

[*Just the opposite.*]

[*You think just the opposite. But you're really trying to do something to me that I don't like.*]

[*What's that?*]

[*You're trying to...you're trying to destroy me.*]

[*No.*]

[*Yes.*]

[*Well you've completely misunderstood what I'm asking these questions for, the Captain said.*]

[*No, I haven't. I've completely understood it just exactly right, Lila said.*] All men do that. You're no big exception. Jerry did it. Every man does it. But you know something? It won't work.

[*I'm not trying to destroy you, he said.*]

[*That's what you think.*] You're just playing around the edges, aren't you! You can't go to the center of me. You don't know where the center of me is!

[That set him back.]

You're not a woman. You don't know. When men make love they're really trying to destroy you. A woman's got to be real quiet inside because if she shows a man anything they'll try to kill it.

But they all get fooled because there's nothing to destroy but what's in their own mind. And so they destroy that and then they hate what's left and they call what's left, 'Lila,' and they hate Lila. But Lila isn't anybody. That's true. You don't believe it, but it's true.

Women are very deep, [*Lila said.*] But men never see it. They're too selfish. They always want women to understand them. And that's all they ever care about. That's why they always have to try to destroy them.

[*I'm just asking questions, the Captain said.*]

Fuck your questions! I'm whatever your questions turn me into. You don't see that. It's your questions that make me who I am. If you think I'm an angel then that's what I am. If you think I'm a whore then that's what I am. I'm whatever you think. And if you change your mind about me then I change too. So whatever Richard tells you, it's true. There's no way he can lie about me.

[*Lila took the bottle and took a swig down straight. The hell with glasses, she said.*] Everybody wants to turn Lila into somebody else. And most women put up with that, because they want the kids and the money and the good-looking clothes. But it won't work with me. I'm just Lila and I always will be. And if men don't like me the way I am, then men can just get out. I don't need them. I don't need anyone. I'll die first. That's just the way I am.

MIDDLE PASSAGE
by Charles Johnson
New Orleans - 1830 - Isadora Baily (20's)

Isadora answers her boyfriend Rutherford's question as to why
she has conspired with his murderous creditors to blackmail him
into marriage with her.

ISADORA: Because I love you...you fool!...and I don't know what
to *do* about it because you don't love *me!* I know that! I'm not
blind, Rutherford. [*She began gathering hairpins off the boardwalk,
sticking them any which way back into her head.*] It's because I'm
not...not pretty. No, don't say it! That *is* why. Because I'm *dark.*
You'd rather have a beautiful, glamorous, light-skinned wife like the
women in the theaters and magazines. It's what all men want,
someone they can show off and say to the world, 'See, look what
I'm humping!' But she'd worry you sorely, Rutherford—I know
that—you'd be suspicious of every man who came to the house, and
your friends too, and she'd be vain and lazy and squander your
money on all sorts of foolish things, and she'd hate having children,
or doing housework, or being at your side when you're sick, but *I*
can make you happy! [*We were drawing a crowd, she noticed, and
lowered her voice, sniffling a little as she tried to push her hat back
into shape.*] I'd hoped that you'd *learn* to love me the way I love
you...
    [*Isadora, I struggled. It's not like that. I do love you. It's just
that I don't want to marry anyone...*]
    Well, you're getting married tomorrow, or I'm taking back my
money. [*Isadora rammed her hat, hopelessly ruined, down over her
ears, her eyes still blazing.*] You choose, Rutherford Calhoun,
whichever way you like.

MIDDLE PASSAGE
by Charles Johnson
Atlantic Ocean - 1830 - Peter Cringle (20's)

Cringle, a finer type than the usual crewman, explains how he
came to be a seafarer.

PETER: Then you're luckier—and freer—than you know. You can
never make a man like my father accept you on your own terms.
Nor can you argue other alternatives with him, because material
success is a pretty tyrannical proof for one's point of view. Truth
is what *works,* pragmatically, in the sphere of commerce. You can't
surpass him, because he's done everything, been everywhere before
you got there, knows everyone, judges everything in terms of profit
and how wide an impression it makes in the world, and hasn't left
you any room to *do* anything except join his legion of admirers.
And, worst of all, you must admire such awesome success as his,
even though he feels, of course, that your mother corrupted you too
much with books and crafts when you were young—it's always the
mother he blames, you know, for spoiling you with poetry, or...
[*He lost track of his thought and rubbed his bladelike nose.*] I'm
here, Rutherford, because if he can't have a son who's a captain of
industry, like himself, or a forceful personality like Falcon—they
were old friends—or his favorite aide in his company, one William
Jenson by name, who is *really* his son in spirit, I believe, one of
those orphans who fashioned himself by his own hand, as my father
says he did, and don't even *ask* me to tell you how it feels to see
him grooming this lad, who looked at me with such self-satisfied
smirks that I could have strangled him...if he can have none of
these, then he wants, I suppose, a ship's captain. Should I fail at
this, there's nothing else, because I shall not go crawling back to
work in his company.

MIDDLE PASSAGE
by Charles Johnson
Atlantic Ocean - 1830's - Squibb (50's)

Aboard a slaver, having suffered a successful mutiny by the
black prisoners, and where everyone is starving and sick, Squibb
explains to a cabin boy from whence derived the meat stew they
have just eaten.

SQUIBB: Yuh had Mr. Cringle fer supper, m'boy. We all did.
Now, lie back, dammit! This was what he wanted. I was sittin'
with him toward the end, which he knew was comin'. Yuh know,
when a body goes the bladder 'n' bowels fly open—I seen it happen
a hundred times—and yer mates have to clean yuh hup and all. He
wanted to spare us that, so he asked the blacks to he'p him to the
head. After he was done, he had a few mates gather round him. By
that time we was eatin' our shoes, barnacles, 'n' the buttons off our
shirts. The women and children had chewed every shred of leather
off the pumps. So Cringle says, in a voice as calm as a chaplain's,
'My friends, I have no inheritance to leave my family in America.
They'll not miss me, I'm sure, but I wish to leave you something,
for no man could ask for better shipmates than thee. You're brave
lads. The lasses have given their full share as bluejackets too, and
methinks 'tis scandalous how some writers such as Amasa Delano
have slandered black rebels in their tales. Of course, I fear you'll
get ptomaine if you put me into a pot, but I've nothing else to give.
I hope this will help. Please, leave me a moment to pray....'
    He took mebbe fifteen minutes. After that he called me in and
give me his knife. Cringle closed me fingers round the handle. He
instructed me that if I preferred not to kill him face to face, he'd
turn his back to me. Don't you know he told me to cover his
mouth, plunge the knife between his shoulder blades, then pull it free
and cut his throat from behind. If that was too difficult for me, he
said I should stab into the soft flesh behind his ear, pokin' straight
through the brain. If not that method, then I was to grip the blade
with both hands and strike just below his collarbone, workin' the

knife back and forth so it wouldn't break when I withdrew it. He told me we was down to only four or five knives, so I couldn't afford to have this one snap off inside him when his body pitched forward.

At first I couldn't do it, Illinois. I started to ask if it wouldn't be better fer us to die like men, but I checked meself before sayin' a thing so foolish, 'cause what could I mean? What was the limit of bein' human? How much could yuh take away and still *be* a man? In a kind of daze I done what he wanted, standin' back from meself, then unstringin' him, and it was in a daze that I lay back, short-winded and watchin' the Africans cut away Cringle's head, hands, feet, and bowels, and throw 'em overboard. Next, they quartered him. They skinned him and cut the meat into spareribs, fatback, bacon, and ham. It was then I reckon it hit me, that I'd killed a man. [*Squibb's eyes darted toward the cabin door, as if the mate's ghost might be standing there.*] I can't sink no lower, laddie, and I 'spect Mr. Cringle's won his wings. After what he done, I don't plan to lose yuh. Yuh kin count on that...

THE NAMES
by Don DeLillo
Greek Islands - Present - Del (20's)

Del, a camerawoman, lives with Frank, a filmmaker. She tells
a friend why she respects Frank.

DEL: Frank is loyal, [*she said*.] He's serious about that. He's got
a side people don't know. He more or less literally saved my life.
He has that side. I wouldn't call it protective exactly. It's a little
deeper. He wanted to show me I could be better than I was. It's
partly because he thought the way I was living was a form of self-
indulgence, which is something he hates. But he also wanted to get
me out of there. I was hanging around with people on the fringes.
They were people with borrowed vans. Everybody had a borrowed
van or knew where to get one. I was always crossing a bridge in
someone's borrowed van. I lived with a van painter for a while.
We lived in his van. He painted mystical designs on vans and
campers. He was after a total design environment, he used to say.
Your house, your van, your garage. That was his vision. I was
working in television then, a fringe job. TV is the coke medium.
The pace is the same. Frank helped me with that. I always half-
disgusted him. How I could think so little of myself that I would
just go to waste.
    [*She used lens tissue moistened with alcohol.*]
    [*When are you going home?*]
    [*When he's ready, she said.*]
    [*Where do you live?*]
    [*Oakland.*]
    [*Where does Frank live?*]
    [*He wouldn't want me to say.*]
    [*He was always like that. Funny. We never knew where he
lived. At least I didn't.*]
    He took me to the hospital to see my father dying. I had to be
dragged if you can picture how pathetic. Do the hard things. That's
a skill I don't ever want to learn.

THE NAMES
by Don DeLillo
Greece - Present - James (30's)

James has become infatuated watching Janet, a slim American, belly dance at a night club. He talks to her at a table, trying to reach her in a very direct and intense way.

JAMES: I'd like to walk out of here with your panties in my back pocket. You'd have to follow me, wouldn't you? I'd like to slip my hand under your blouse and detach your bra. I want to sit here and talk to you knowing I've got your bra and panties in my pocket. That's all I ask. The knowledge of a bareness under your clothes. Knowing that, sitting here talking to you and knowing you were naked under your clothes, this would enable me to live another ten years, this knowledge alone, independent of food and drink. Are you wearing a bra in fact? I'm not one of those men who can tell at a glance. I've never had the self-assured powers of observation that would allow me to say that this or that woman was or was not wearing a bra. As a kid I never stood on street corners and estimated cup measurements. There goes a C cup, like that, with total self-assurance.
[*Please. I think I ought to go.*]
Only to put my hands under your clothes. No more than that. What we did as kids, adolescent sex, how happy that would make me. A back room in your family's summer bungalow. A mildewed room, a darkening, a sudden rain. Move against me, push me off, pull me onto you again. Worried about someone coming back, back from the lake, the yard sale. Worried about everything we're doing. The rain loosens every fresh smell in the countryside. It comes in on us from outdoors, rain-fresh, rain-washed, lovely, sweet-smelling, a chill in the summer air. It's nature, it's sex. And you pull me onto you and worry and tell me not to, not to.

THE POWER OF ONE
by Bryce Courtenay
South Africa - 1950 - Peekay (10)

Peekay, a farm boy, having just been sent to a boys' boarding
school, tells of his welcome.

PEEKAY: I had had no previous warning that I was wicked and it
came as a fearful surprise. I was blubbing to myself in the little
kids' dormitory when suddenly I was dragged from under my horrid
camphor-smelling blanket by two eleven-year-olds and taken to the
seniors' dormitory to stand trial before the council of war.

My trial, of course, was a travesty of justice. But then, what
could I expect? I had been caught deep behind enemy lines and
everyone, even a five-year-old, knows this means the death sentence.
I stood gibbering, unable to understand the language of the stentorian
twelve-year-old judge, or the reason for the hilarity when sentence
was passed. But I guessed the worst.

I wasn't quite sure what death was. I knew it was something
that happened on the farm in the slaughterhouse to pigs and goats
and an occasional heifer. The squeal from the pigs was so awful that
I knew it wasn't much of an experience, even for pigs.

And I knew something else for sure; death wasn't as good as
life. Now death was about to happen to me before I could really get
the hang of life. Trying hard to hold back my tears, I was dragged
off.

It must have been a full moon that night because the shower
room was bathed in blue light. The stark granite walls of the shower
recesses stood sharply angled against the wet cement floor. I had
never been in a shower room before, and this place resembled the
slaughterhouse on the farm. It even smelled the same, of urine and
blue carbolic soap, so I guessed this was where my death would take
place.

My eyes were a bit swollen from crying but I could see where
the meat hooks were supposed to hang. Each granite slab had a pipe
protruding from the wall behind it, with a knob on the end. They

would suspend me from one of these and I would be dead, just like the pigs.

I was told to remove my pajamas and to kneel inside the shower recess facing the wall. I looked directly down into the hole in the floor where all the blood would drain away.

I closed my eyes and said a silent, sobbing prayer. My prayer wasn't to God, but to my nanny. It seemed the more urgent thing to do. When she couldn't solve a problem for me, she'd say, "We must ask Inkosi-Inkosikazi, the great medicine man, he will know what to do." Although we never actually called on the services of the great man, it didn't seem to matter; it was comforting to know he was available when needed.

Magdalena, a travelling actress/"sensualist," includes in her entourage her precocious twelve-year-old niece Maud, her dog, and her maid and alter ego, Clara. A boating accident claims Clara's life and injures Magdalena's face. Maud is saved by a gallant fifteen-year-old, Daniel Quinn. When Maud professes her eternal love for young Quinn, Magdalena delivers a stern lecture to her.

MAGDALENA: How dare you put your life in such jeopardy? [*said the angry Magdalena.*] How dare you, when I am so hounded by fate. Clara, my own sweet serving girl, uselessly drowned, my face almost the ruination of us all, for where would any of us be without it? And you, spiteful child, you take it upon yourself to starve your body, your only salvation. Do you think men care for a woman's mind, especially the mind of a wicked twelve-year-old like you? Do you think you can live by your wits alone, with no help from the talents you inherited with your flesh? Do you think that silly canal boy can save you from ruination, when he cannot even save himself? He's a penniless orphan, seeking to steal you away from me with his urchin ways. [*(This remark cut me deeply.)*]

[*You fail to see in him the high quality I see, said Maud (and I recovered immediately from La Ultima's cut.)*]

Child, [*said the courtesan,*] you have a strong mind, but you are little schooled in the ways of men. And now it is *you* who must take Clara's place as my social companion. It is *you* whom I must dress as I dress myself. It is early for you, but this is an inheritance we must learn to accept.

[*You want me to love men for money? asked Maud.*]

I shall teach you to talk to men, to disarm them of their harsh moods, to entice them into sweetness, to pleasure them. I shall turn you into a songbird, a dancing swan. I shall teach you how to survive this life, child Maudie.

QUINN'S BOOK
by William Kennedy
Albany, NY - 1850 - Joey Ryan (14)

Joey Ryan, his father, sister and mother are recent immigrants to America. His father has just been killed by a drunken man who, having been laid off at the foundry, looks for a newly hired man to take vengeance on. When asked where he came from in Ireland, Joey answers.

JOEY: From a ditch near Cashel, [*he said.*] The landlord tumbled our house and put us off our land, and me father piled all we owned in a cart and we pushed it till we couldn't climb the hill. Then we lived in the ditch and used the wagon as a roof. We could see the Galty Mountains from the ditch. They tumbled our house to make room for the landlord's cows. 'They're in grave need of pasture,' the landlord told me pa. Then we left the ditch, threw things away to lighten our load, and the three of us hauled the cart up the mountain, a terrible high mountain of four hundred feet it was, and me sister settin' the block at the wheel. We done it at last and got over the mountain, but goin' down the back side was near as troublesome as goin' up the front, and we almost lost the cart two or three assorted times. We begged food, and when we couldn't get any we stole it, or we ate grass. Then we went to me uncle's place on the road to Tipperary, and he took us in and paid for Pa to go to America. Pa himself is all of us that went over. The night before he left we had a wake for his leavin', with me ma keenin' for hours over his goin'. 'Ye won't come back for us,' she kept saying. It was near to bury him, is what it was. But he sent remittances and got us all over here, me and me sister and me mother. And didn't we all come to this town of Albany, because we couldn't fit in New York in the wee room Pa lived in. We was here just a few weeks and no money left when he got the foundry job, and then, a little after that, they broke his skull, the man did, the bastard man.

QUINN'S BOOK
by William Kennedy
Albany, NY - 1864 - Daniel Quinn (29)

Daniel Quinn, addressing an audience of local people eager to
know about the war firsthand, relates a very personal war
experience.

DANIEL: I got my own reality the day I was hit by a spent reb can-
nonball. Just touched by it, really, and it wasn't moving very fast.
But it knocked me down, broke my leg and made me bleed, and I
thought maybe I'd die alone there on the battlefield. I couldn't even
give a good explanation of why I was hit. The battle was long over
and I wasn't a soldier. I was just out there looking for survivors and
some reb cannoneer maybe figured, why not wipe out that Yankee
bastard? He let one go I never paid any attention to, and it got me.
I might be out there yet, but then along came this grayback doctor
and I see him working on hurt rebs. I called out, 'Hey, doc, can
you stop my bleeding and set my leg?' And he said, 'I cain't set no
laigs. I got soldiers of my own dyin' here.' And he went on
helping rebs. So I called out and said, 'Hey, doc, I got money I can
pay you if you stop my bleeding and set my leg.' And the doc looks
me over and says, 'How much you got, son?' and I say, 'I got
twenty-five dollars in gold I been savin' for my retirement,' and he
says, 'Okay, I can help you retire.' And he comes over and looks
me up and down and says, 'Where's the gold?' And I fished in my
money belt and showed it to him, and he smiled nice as peach pie at
me and went ahead and stitched me up and put a splint on me, and
then he wrapped that leg so fine I got right up and started to walk.
I gave him the gold and says to him, 'Thanks a lot, doc,' just like
he was a human being. And he says, 'Don't mention it, son, but
don't put too much pressure on that leg,' just like I was some
goddamned reb.

QUINN'S BOOK
by William Kennedy
Albany, NY - 1864 - Daniel Quinn (29)

Daniel Quinn, addressing an audience of his hometown people,
talks of a local boy who didn't make good during the war.

DANIEL: We called him Peaches Plum, [*said Quinn,*] and he was
never worth much in any context you might want to discuss. He
was one of your neighbors, and he and I went to school together
here fifteen, twenty years ago. We were in Virginia, and we heard
the drum corps beating a muffled Dead March in the woods near us
and we all knew what was coming. Before long, orders came down
to form with the whole First Division, and the Forty-fourth moved
out onto elevated ground, facing an open field. The men formed a
line, division front, facing five fresh graves.

That, my friends, was a fearful sight. Also very rousing somehow, with all those brass buttons and rifles shining in the sun, and
kids watching from trees, and older men alone on horses, or on top
of rooves, and everybody's eye on Peaches and four other boys as
they came walking: two, two, and one. Peaches was the one,
walking behind the drum corps, and followed by the provost guard,
fifty of them with bayonets fixed. Five clergymen walked along,
too, reading scriptures, and thirty pallbearers carried five new
coffins. The procession went up and back the length of the whole
line of battle and then the pallbearers stopped at the fresh graves.
The five prisoners stopped, too, and stood there with their hands
tied, a guard alongside each one of them. Then those five young
men sat down on their coffins.

I never got to talk privately with Peaches, but I dug up his story,
once I saw it was him. Never wrote it, though, and I'm only telling
it now because Will Canaday says you folks are hounds for reality.

Peaches was a bounty jumper who joined the army eighteen
times. You only got a fifty-dollar bounty for joining up when
Peaches started his jumping career. Used to be there was enough
henpecked husbands, and third sons, and boys who got girls in

69

trouble, who were glad to go to war and improve their outlook. But the war kept on going and volunteers fell away to a trickle, and so the price of bounties went up, all the way to a thousand dollars, which is what they're paying right now. Peaches, he made lots of money enlisting but he never got to keep it. When he'd light out he'd always bring the cash back home to his pa, like he was supposed to. Then one day after the draft came in, Peaches's pa told him, 'Go join up the army again, Peaches, only this time don't come back because you're going in place of your brother.' This brother was a lawyer, a son the father couldn't do without, the way he could do without Peaches.

All those times Peaches joined up he never got close to a battle. He'd just disappear during the night off a train, or on a march toward some regiment, then head back home to Pa. But this time Peaches finally went to war. He saw a lot of corpses and didn't want to become one of those, so he drew on his talents and his instincts, and he took out for points north. And he ran right into another unit and got court-martialed for desertion along with the four other boys who ran with him. They were all found guilty and the President approved they be shot as a warning to cowards and mercenary men in the army. I guess we all know how many good soldiers have the impulse to run, but somehow don't, either out of fear, or good sense, or because they want to kill rebs. One youngster told me, 'I'm stickin' because we got justice on our side.' Lot of rebs think the same way, but that doesn't matter. Death's all that matters, and I know you all want the reality of that, just like the folks back home in the real olden days who wanted to know how their war was going. And their soldiers would collect the heads and genitals of the enemy and bring 'em back home for inspection to prove the army was doing its job. Peaches never got into any of that kind of fun. He was just one of those poor souls who fumble their way through life, never quite knowing the rules, never playing by them even if they think they know them, always fated to be a pawn of other folks.

Poor Peaches. Grizzled men around me were crying as the provost guard took up its position, ten guardsmen for each of the five prisoners, rifles ready, standing about fifteen yards away, while the captain of the guard read the five orders of execution out loud. The clergy came by and talked to each of the prisoners for a few minutes, and then the officers started putting those white blindfolds on the chosen five.

I could see Peaches really clear, see him crying and quaking, and before I knew what I was doing I'd called out, 'So long, Peaches, and good luck,' which wasn't very appropriate, I admit, but that's what I said. Peaches looked toward my voice and nodded his head. 'Okay,' he yelled. Then his blindfold was on, the black cap was placed over his face, and it was ready, aim, fire. Four of the prisoners fell backward onto their coffins. Peaches took the bullets and didn't let them knock him over. He crumpled in place and I never felt more an outsider in this life. All that pomp and panoply in service of five more corpses. It's a question, I'll tell you. But that's all that's left in me—a kind of fatal quizzicality, you might call it. I hope my sharing it with you has been of some value.

ROGER'S VERSION
by John Updike
A New England College Town - Present - Mr. Kohler (19-20)

Kohler, a college physics major, attempts to convince Roger Lambert, a divinity professor, of the scientific basis of the existence of God. He is seeking support for a grant application for money to support research into his theory.

KOHLER: The sun. Yellow stars like the sun, to give off so much steady heat for ten billion years or so, are balanced like on a knife edge between the inward pull of gravity and the outward push of thermonuclear reaction. If the gravitational coupling constant were any smaller, they'd balloon and all be blue giants; any smaller, they'd shrivel and be red dwarves. A blue giant doesn't last long enough for life to evolve, and the red dwarf radiates too weakly to ever get it started. Everywhere you look, [*he instructed me,*] there are these terrifically finely adjusted constants that have to be just what they are, or there wouldn't be a world we could recognize, and there's no intrinsic reason for those constants to be what they are except to say *God made them that way.* God made Heaven and Earth. It's what science has come to. Believe me.

ROGER'S VERSION
by John Updike
A New England College Town - Present - Verna (early 20's)

*Verna describes her situation and living conditions to her uncle,
who has come to see her unexpectedly.*

VERNA: This project is half old dagos and half black dudes you
say 'Hi' to in the hall they think you want to get screwed. These
guys, they can smell when you've been nicked, even without seeing
Paula. Then they want to put you out on the street; their idea of a
great success in life is pimping for a string of white girls. It really
is. [*Her slant eyes went watery.*] My parents were right, I guess;
I've backed myself into this horrible corner. I'm lonely, I'm lonely
all the time, can't just talk to anybody like a man can, it gets to be
a negotiation. And last night 'Dynasty' was on so I don't even have
that to look forward to for a week.

ROGER'S VERSION
by John Updike

A New England College Town - Present - Verna (early 20's)

Verna suddenly believes that her uncle's unexpected interest in her welfare is based on his concern for her baby daughter, Paula.

VERNA: So that's who this mercy call is all about. Little honey chile. Save your charity, Nunc, she can take care of herself. All the little bitch does all day is bug me. I sit out there in the playground for hours while she eats broken glass. But it never kills her, all that happens is her shit sparkles. [*She laughed again, at her own joke. I let myself smile. She wiped her stubby, shiny nose. Without that nose, and if she had lost ten pounds, she might have been pretty.*] On top of everything else, I'm getting a fucking cold. You wonder why everybody doesn't commit suicide sometimes.

THE SECRET PILGRIM
by John le Carré
London - 1960's - Smiley (60's)

Here, Smiley, a Secret Service agent, lectures a class of novice spies.

SMILEY: Now do please remember, [*Smiley piously exhorted his young audience, in much the tone he might have selected if he had been asking them to put their offerings in the collection box as they were leaving,*] that the privately educated English- man—and Englishwoman, if you will allow me—is the greatest dissembler on earth. [*He waited for the laughter to subside.*] Was, is now and ever shall be for as long as our disgraceful school system remains intact. Nobody will charm you so glibly, disguise his feelings from you better, cover his tracks more skillfully or find it harder to confess to you that he's been a damned fool. Nobody acts braver when he's frightened stiff, or happier when he's miserable; nobody can flatter you better when he hates you than your extrovert Englishman or woman of the supposedly privileged classes. He can have a Force Twelve nervous breakdown while he stands next to you in the bus queue, and you may be his best friend, but you'll never be the wiser. Which is why some of our best officers turn out to be our worst. And our worst, our best. And why the most difficult agent you will ever have to run is yourself.

THE SECRET PILGRIM
by John le Carré
Cambodian jungle - 1960's - Hansen (40's)

Here Hansen tells a fellow spy of his daughter Marie and how
he discovered she had been captured by the Khmer Rouge.

HANSEN: While I was still a priest, I visited the temples of
Cambodia, [*he said.*] While I was there, I fell in love with a
village woman and made her pregnant. In Cambodia it was the best
time still. Sihanouk ruled. I remained with her until the child was
born. A girl. I christened her Marie. I gave the mother money and
returned to Djakarta, but I missed my child terribly. I sent more
money. I sent money to the headman to look after them. I sent
letters. I prayed for the child and her mother, and swore that one
day I would care for them properly. As soon as I returned to
Cambodia, I put the mother in my house, even though in the
intervening years she had lost her beauty. My daughter had a
Khmer name, but from the day she came to me I called her Marie.
She liked that. She was proud to have me as her father.

[*He seemed concerned to make clear to me that Marie was at
ease with her European name. It was not an American name, he
said. It was European.*]

I had other women in my household, but Marie was my only
child and I loved her. She was more beautiful than I had imagined
her. But if she had been ugly and ungracious I would have loved
her no less. [*His voice acquired sudden strength and, as I heard it,
warning.*] No woman, no man, no child, ever claimed my love in
such a way. You may say that Marie is the only woman I have
loved purely except for my mother. [*He was staring at me in the
darkness, challenging me to doubt his passion. But under Hansen's
spell, I doubted nothing and had forgotten everything about myself,
even my own mother's death. He was assuming me, occupying me.*]

Once you have embarked upon the impossible concept of God,
you will know that real love permits no rejection. Perhaps that is
something only a sinner can properly understand. Only a sinner

knows the scale of God's forgiveness.

[*I think I nodded wisely. I thought of Colonel Jerzy. I was wondering why Hansen needed to explain that he could not reject his daughter. Or why his sinfulness was a concern to him when he spoke of her.*]

That evening when I drove home from the temple, there were no children waiting for me in the kampong, though it was the dry season. I was disappointed because we had made a good find that day and I wanted to tell Marie about it. They must be having a school festival, I thought, but I could not think which one. I drove up the hill to the compound and called her name. The compound was empty. The gatehouse empty. The women's cookpots empty under the stilts. I called Marie again, then my wife. Then anybody. No one came. I drove back to the village. I went into the house of one of Marie's friends, then another and another, calling Marie. Even the pigs and chickens had disappeared. I looked for blood, for traces of fighting. There were none. But I found footprints leading into the jungle. I drove back to the compound. I took a spade and cached my radio in the forest, halfway between two tall trees that made a line due west, close to an old ant-hill shaped like a man. I hated all my work for you, all my lies, for you and for the Americans. I still do. I walked back to the house, uncached my codepads and equipment and destroyed them. I was glad to. I hated them also. I put on boots and filled a rucksack with food for a week. With my revolver I sent three bullets through the jeep's engine to immobilise it; then I followed the footprints into the jungle. The jeep was an insult to me, because you had bought it.

[*Alone, Hansen had set off in pursuit of the Khmer Rouge. Other men—even men who were not Western spies—might have thought twice and a third time, even with their wife and daughter taken hostage. Not Hansen. Hansen had one thought and, absolutist that he was, he acted on it.*]

I could not allow myself to be separated from God's grace.

THE SECRET PILGRIM
by John le Carré
Cambodia - 1960's - Marie (late teens)

Here, Hansen's daughter Marie, having been captured and indoctrinated by the Khmer Rouge, identifies her father as a spy after he has been captured.

MARIE: The spy Hansen kept a radio in his house which he used for signalling to the imperialist bombers. Also the names he has mentioned in his confession are fictitious. They are taken from a bourgeois English song which he sang to me when he was pretending to be my father. Also he received imperialist soldiers at our house at night and led them into the jungle. Also he has failed to mention that he has an English mother.

[*The student appeared disappointed. What else has he failed to mention? he asked, flattening a fresh page with the edge of his small hand.*]

During his confinement, he has been guilty of many breaches of regulation. He has hoarded food and attempted to buy the collaboration of comrades in his plans to escape.

[*The student sighed and made more notes. What else has he failed to mention? he asked patiently.*]

He has been wearing his foot chains improperly. When the chains were being fastened, he braced his feet illegally, leaving the chains loose for his escape.

[*Until that moment Hansen had managed to persuade himself that Marie was playing a cunning game. No longer. The game was the reality.*]

He is a whoremonger! [*she screamed through her tears.*] He debauches our women by bringing them to his house and drugging them! He pretends to make a bourgeois marriage, then forces his wife to tolerate his decadent practices! He sleeps with girls of my own age! He pretends he is the father of our children and that our blood is not Khmer! He reads us bourgeois literature in Western languages in order to deprave us! He seduces us by taking us for rides in his jeep and singing imperialist songs to us!

[*He had never heard he scream before. Nor evidently had the student, who appeared embarrassed. But she would not be checked. She persisted in denying him. She told how he had forbidden her mother to love her. She was expressing a hatred for him that he knew was unfeigned, as absolute and inordinate as his love for her. Her body shook with the pent-up hatred of a misused woman, her features were crumpled with hatred and guilt. Her arm struck out and she pointed at him in the classic posture of accusation. Her voice belonged to someone he had never known.*]

Kill him! [*she screamed.*] Kill the despoiler of our people! Kill the corrupter of our Khmer blood! Kill the Western liar who tells us we are different from one another! Avenge the people!

SKINNY LEGS AND ALL
by Tom Robbins
New York City - Present - Reverend Buddy Winkler (40's)

Buddy has run into his twenty-four-year-old niece Ellen Cherry
on a street in New York. He has come on a fundamentalist
"mission." She asks him why he objects to peace in the Middle
East. Buddy answers.

BUDDY: I'll explain right now.

[*No. Please.*]

I'll explain here and now. If you'd been readin' your Scripture,
you'd have knowed the answer. It's not God's plan for there to be
peace in the Middle East. Not yet, it ain't. First, we'll be witness
to an impressive scene. Yea, I say unto you...

[*Oh, shit, she thought. The sax was out of its case.*]

...the awfulness of the impending judgment will be unequaled on
the earth! The Holy Land, your so-called Middle East, is prophesied
to be the scene of the ultimate world war. Combatants will be lured
to the area by demons sent by Satan to assemble the armies of the
world to challenge the armies of heaven. Up and down the Holy
Land, they'll battle. On the very day of the return of Christ, there'll
be house-to-house fighting in Jerusalem itself, the homes ransacked
and the women raped. Zechariah, fourteen, two.

[*Bud, really.*]

This is to be the last war, darlin'. The wicked will be destroyed
once and for all, whereupon the righteous will dwell with Christ in
the New Jerusalem for—

[*Bud!*]

Come on now, let me answer your question. It's not a matter
of us Christians not wantin' peace, it's a matter of the time not bein'
ripe for peace. First, our Messiah must return. Then, the fightin'
in the Holy Land must begin in earnest. These bleedin' hearts
who're clamoring for peace in the Middle East understand not what
they do. They're uninformed troublemakers, interferin' with—and
slowin' down—the natural chain of events that'll fulfill God's
promise and make the world sweet as pie for eternity.

SKINNY LEGS AND ALL
by Tom Robbins
New York City - Present - Boomer Petway (20's)

Boomer has left his wife, Ellen Cherry. Although it is she who
has studied art and come to New York to show, it is Boomer
who has made it big in the New York art scene. Ellen Cherry
didn't go to his opening. She calls to explain why. Boomer
won't talk to her and here explains why.

BOOMER: Horseshit, Ellen Cherry. We never talked. We traded
wisecracks. Wisecracking is not talking.
 [*She started to refute him, but couldn't muster any ready
evidence to support her objection. While she was trying to remember
the last time they'd had a heart-to-heart, he broke the silence with
an outburst.*] You know how come we never talked? 'Cause you
never believed I *could* talk. Not on your level. I couldn't talk about
art. I didn't understand art. I didn't, in fact, give a big rat's ass
about art. And in your opinion, that made me inferior, you know;
some kind of second-class citizen like all those other clods in
Colonial Pines...
 [*No! You were different. And I loved you.*]
 You never loved me. You never. You loved to the left of me
and to the right of me, maybe. You loved above me and underneath
and in back of me somewheres. But you didn't love me. You loved
my biceps and my big ol' welder's cock, and the way I danced and
the way I was looser and more free than you. That's what the hell
you loved. It turned you on that I could be uninhibited, because the
only place *you're* free is on a piece of canvas. In art, you can break
loose of your restraints. Otherwise, you're tight as the peel on a
turnip.

81

SKINNY LEGS AND ALL
by Tom Robbins
New York City - Present - Buddy Winkler (40's)

Buddy is a small-town fundamentalist preacher. Upon hearing
that he and his zealots plan to blow up the Dome of the Rock in
Jerusalem to hasten the advent of Armageddon, Ellen Cherry
accuses Buddy of gambling with the lives of billions of people.
He responds.

BUDDY: Hold on. You jes' hold on now, little miss bleedin'
heart. It ain't a gamble. The word of God is not no lottery ticket.
It shall come to pass. Shall! His admonitions are as plain as the
nose on your painted face. And sure it's gonna be horrible. The
Lord God designed it to be horrible. But the righteous'll come out
of it jes' fine, thank you. Jesus'll gather unto him the faithful to his
breast, and they'll enjoy sweet everlastin' life. Them burns will
heal, and them sores will vanish away. As for your careless and
wicked, they'll jes' be gittin' what's due to 'em. They've had their
fair chance, they'll burn by their own iniquity. So let the war
trumpets sound. Let the missiles rain. It's God's will, and he'll
decide who's innocent and who ain't, not you or the ACLU.

A SOLDIER OF THE GREAT WAR
by Mark Helprin
Rome - 1913 - Orfeo Quatta (60's)

Orfeo, a hunchback dwarf and madman, speaks to a sold-out auditorium in Bologna in the guise of the president of the University of Trondheim in Norway.

ORFEO: I miss my home in Trondheim,   [*he said in an astoundingly authoritative, quasi-governmental, contra-basso.*]   I miss the way the arctic winds push the icicles from the eaves, and how they shatter as they fall, like a bomb exploding in a city of glass.

[*The audience came to attention in its seats. What it didn't know was that as Orfeo spoke in his deep contra-basso his soul was swaying to the music of the circus.*]

You don't know anything about the sap, [*he said.*] You haven't the vaguest idea of the blessed sap, the most gracious sap that fills the bone-white valley of the moon.

[*His listeners pulled themselves up ramrod straight, their brows knit, trying to accommodate his pronouncements.*]

You little snot-noses, baboons. You look like the monkeys on the Rock of Gibraltar.

[*Their hearts thudded, they could feel the blood massing in their aortas, and they were as tense as crickets. He went on, growing more and more relaxed, his ease the inverse function of their tightening stomachs.*]

All my life I've suffered this deformity while you sat in your parents' well appointed kitchens stuffing zabaglione into your gorgeous bodies—the girls, sunburnt and green-eyed, with thick tresses of blond hair braided in lascivious basket weave that fell across their strong backs....

The boys, stupid granite-jawed idiots twice my height, intoxicated with their handsomeness, simply arrived in the afternoon, played tennis, ate, and coasted into delicious nudity with those beautiful, perfectly formed women.

83

A SOLDIER OF THE GREAT WAR

I knew even before I had desire that it would be gnarled and knotted, black and hard, a tree that would never bear fruit, a fish that would never jump, a cat that would never meow. All my life, bitterness and regret, bitterness, and regret.

And yet, [*he said, briefly closing his eyes,*] I was able to imagine the softness and sweetness of love, for a time.

A SOLDIER OF THE GREAT WAR
by Mark Helprin
Italy - 1916 - Guariglia (30's)
Guariglia is an imprisoned army deserter awaiting execution.
He is a devoted father and here responds to his friend who refers
to clouds as rafts for souls.

GUARIGLIA: I would like that, [*Guariglia said.*] I'd prefer to
stay nearby and look down, to pass over Rome. It sounds to me a
little better than all the stuff about being in the stars, because you
wouldn't be able to breathe up there, and it would be either too
bright or too dark. In the clouds, on the other hand, ah, that would
be nice.

[*Yes, Fabio added, innocently. You would be able to see your
children. You could paddle over Rome and check on them now and
then.*]

I'm going to write a letter to my children and tell them to look
for me there, [*Guariglia said.*] Even if it's not true, it's a good
way to remember.

A few days ago, my youngest, who is two and a half, refused to
go to bed. She cried so hard she choked for air. My wife said leave
her, it's the only thing to do if you don't want to ruin a child.

But in my daughter's cries I heard that she was hurt. I picked
her up and held her. I couldn't help it. I find it almost impossible
to be hard with her: I didn't see her for the first two years of her
life. It took fifteen minutes for her to stop gasping for air. As soon
as she'd stop for a moment, she'd start up again. She was red, her
face was swollen, and she pounded my chest with her fists. Because
she was so hot—she sleeps in a kind of sack that my wife made for
her, which is very warm—I took her up to the roof, and she stopped
crying. I don't think she'd ever seen the night sky. There's a war
on, I told her, but the sky is still there, the stars are still there.

She loved them, she really did, and while she held on to my
neck and stared up at the sky, half an hour passed. You could
almost hear the dark clouds moving overhead. I know that something up there spoke to the soul of my child, so perhaps Alessandro
is right. Perhaps the clouds are the rafts of souls.

A SOLDIER OF THE GREAT WAR
by Mark Helprin
Alpines, Italy - 1916 - General (30's)

Here, a general speaks to his troops before sending them into battle in the mountains between Italy and Austria.

GENERAL: You may wonder how I can ask you to die so that we can take apart their layer cake, especially when you and I know that no matter what we do, the mountains will soon be silent. How is it that, if you turn from this meaningless task, I will have you shot?

It's rather simple. If I turn from this unpleasant task, I, too, will be shot. So it goes all the way to the top, and you know as well as I that the chiefs of the people, if they surrender, are shot by the people they would shoot for surrendering.

This is a conundrum easily resolved by shooting only the people on the other side, and that's how war goes on and on. Though the whole world may have gone mad, we are going to regain our sanity, gradually and fully, by means of a slow and rewarding fiction. I am asking you to go to Innsbruck. Every meter will be contested, and for every meter, someone will die, but we are going to regain our sanity by vesting in each particle of ground an artificial value. It has been done throughout history with metals and spices. Merchants assess their lives in numbers, and they are almost always saner than those who set out to seek the truth. Like merchants, we will peg our sanity to artificial standards—land taken, and days alive.

I'm responsible to Rome for capturing ground, and I cannot change that. I'm responsible to you for keeping you alive, and that I will not change. I do my best to balance the two. We don't practice the same carnage up here as they do lower down. It's the terrain, the thin air, and our relative lack of mass. And the north is not infinity, for the mountains stop, and then you're in Germany. If you survive, you'll be able to remember having been there. You'll recall it fifty years from now, in some quiet place, surrounded by children, not a single one knowing the folly to which you were committed, and all sweetly ready to commit it anew.

A SOLDIER OF THE GREAT WAR

[*He hesitated.*] And if you don't ever leave this place...Well, the air is magical here, and so is the sudden darkness, and so is the chill. In the daytime, in the light, with the sky changing, nothing is quite as alive. At night or in storms it seems like the tunnel to death. Don't misinterpret me. I want that tunnel so crowded with the braying enemy that no room will be left for us, but, should you not make it back to a table in the piazza, you will have died in the best place for dying the world has ever known. What I mean is, here, you're practically at the gates.

A SOLDIER OF THE GREAT WAR
by Mark Helprin
Austria - 1917 - Field Marshal Strassnitzky (50's)

Strassnitzky explains to his Italian prisoner Alessandro why he is a pacifist.

STRASSNITZKY: I'm a pacifist.

[*A pacifist!*]

When I was in school, [*Strassnitzky said,*] I went out one morning in my riding clothes and shod in heavy boots, and as I left the last step I came down on a young bird that had been resting at the foot of the stairs, having been savaged by a hawk. My weight on it pushed the air out of its lungs, and when I turned to see what had made that unearthly noise, the bird looked at me in such a way that I knew that even animals have souls. Only a creature with a soul could have had eyes so expressive and so understanding, and I had crushed it as it lay dying. It took a full day to die, and since then I have been what is called a pacifist. The term is inexact and demeaning, for a pacifist has no peace in his soul, and he knows rage as much as anyone else, but he simply will not kill.

A SOLDIER OF THE GREAT WAR
by Mark Helprin
Italian Countryside - 1960's - Alessandro (70's)

Alessandro tells his young friend Nicolo how he found his love
after the great war.

ALESSANDRO: Ariane was indeed the woman I saw just before
the house was bombed, but my conception of time was wrong. She
had run down two flights of stairs, and was rushing out to meet me,
but stretchers were blocking the hallway that led to the front, so she
turned to go out the back. She heard the bomb smash through the
roof. She said it sounded like a basket being broken up before it's
thrown away. It pierced the ceilings of the third, second, and first
floors. She remembered that this sounded like cards being shuffled.

It exploded in the front room, and the impact pushed the interior
walls, in one piece, against the outside walls of the building, which
then collapsed upon itself. At the instant of detonation Ariane was
at the open door, and the air compressing inside blew her ten meters
from the house. She landed on the grass, where she lay paralyzed
and hardly able to breathe. Everyone else inside had been crushed,
burned, obliterated.

And then, suddenly, in Rome, on a calm day in June, she was
standing in front of me, in a towel. I held her....I wouldn't let go.
It must have been an hour. She couldn't speak, because every time
she tried to say something, she wept. The towel slipped and she was
naked in my arms. Though the cousin was amazed, Paolo, our son,
held tightly to his mother's neck, because of her tears, and paid no
heed to the scandalous circumstances.

She cried. Within her crying, sometimes, she laughed, but not
much, and the baby cried and stroked her head, and I, I was
overcome, but though I was overcome I thought back upon the
painting, and my God, Ariane was naked with a child in her arms,
and I had found her, and I could not believe it, but it was true, it
was certainly true, and if you ask me how or why it happened I can't
tell you, but life and death have a rhythm, an alternating rhythm,

and you never know what to expect, as it is in God's hands, and I was waiting for a thunderstorm, for the sky to darken, for lightning, and wind. We were as stunned as the people in the Bible upon whom miracles are showered, and even though the thunderstorm did not come until the next night, each and every lightning flash, and each and every thundercrack, was a triumph.

A TASTE FOR DEATH
by P.D. James
London - Present - Evelyn Matlock (40)

During a murder investigation, Inspector Dalgliesh's subordinate Massingham accuses the maid of having an affair with the master of the house. Lady Ursula characterizes the accusation as ridiculous and grotesque. Evelyn responds.

EVELYN: Why is it ridiculous, why is it grotesque? You can't bear to believe it, can you? You've had lovers enough in your time, everyone knows that. You're notorious. Well, you're old now, crippled and ugly and no one wants you, man or woman, and you can't bear to think that someone might want me. Well, he did and he does. He loves me. We love each other. He cares. He knows what my life is like in this house. I'm tired, I'm overworked and I hate you all. You didn't know that, did you? You thought I was grateful. Grateful for the job of washing you like a baby, grateful for waiting on a woman too idle to pick up her own underclothes from the floor, grateful for the worst bedroom in the house, grateful for a home, a bed, a roof, the next meal. This place isn't a home. It's a museum. It's dead. It's been dead for years. And you think of no one but yourselves. Do this, Mattie, fetch that, Mattie, run my bath, Mattie. I do have a name. He calls me Evelyn. Evelyn, that's my name. I'm not a cat or a dog, I'm not a household pet.

VANISHED
by Mary McGarry Morris
Fairground - Present - Canny (7)

Canny was stolen as an infant by Dotty and Wallace, whom she
now knows as her parents. They live the life of hobos. Canny
finds her Poppy (Wallace) in the parking lot of an amusement
park and explains why she's late.

CANNY: We had slush and fried dough, [*Canny was saying.*] And
then we went on the Wonder Whip and then after, we went on the
Leaping Lizard. It kinda wiggled fast like this, [*she illustrated with
her hand.*] Then it went, woop! Like this, [*she said, snapping her
hand up in the air,*] then down. And that's when I threw up. On
one of the downs. So I told Momma I was too sick to go on any
more rides and she felt real bad. 'Specially 'cause of the Black
Hole. It has shooting stars and space music so we watched for a
while and Momma kept teasing me to try it. She said it's built
special, the way they do space ships for astronauts, and she said how
they never get space sick now, do they—so acourse, I wouldn't get
sick.... [*She shrugged again, only this time it was more like a
shiver. Her voice grew shrill.*] Then these two guys in cowboy hats
came up the ramp. And Momma was starting to get mad at me.
She kept saying how I promised her all day I'd go on the rides and
how I was always breaking promises and it wasn't fair. Then one
of the guys laughed and he said Momma sounded like the little girl
and I sounded like the mother. [*Canny laughed uneasily.*] And
Momma said, 'Well, that's kinda how it goes.' And then one of the
guys said he'd do the Black Hole with Momma and I could stand and
wait with his friend on the ramp. So I did and then when they came
out, the guy with me went in with Momma and the first guy stayed.
He put me up on the railing and he put his hand someplace,
Poppy....

VANISHED
by Mary McGarry Morris
Massachusetts - Present - Dotty (20's)

Dotty, Wallace and seven-year-old Canny have been "on the road" for five years. Here, Dotty tells her new friend Huller, an ex-con, how she kidnapped Canny.

DOTTY: I was gonna tell whoever came to the door I was collecting for cancer or something and then when nobody came, I just opened the door and went inside, straight on into the kitchen. There was a glass jar on the counter with dimes in it and then all of a sudden I remembered how hungry I was and I opened the fridge and stood there looking in at all the food, and then I heard this baby voice saying, 'Hi, hi,' and over the door of the fridge, I could see this tiny little girl. She was in the other room, in her playpen, you know, with her face pressed to the side, all cute and pudgy through the holes. The phone started to ring and she kept saying, 'Hi, hi,' louder and louder like she wanted me to say it back. Like if I didn't, she'd cry or something. So I went in and I said, 'Hi.' And then when I started to go, she started hollering it, 'Hi! Hi!'

[*Dotty drew her knees to her chin and smiled. Wallace was looking at her now, and listening carefully.*]

She wouldn't shut up and then the phone stopped ringing, so I grabbed her and then I thought I heard footsteps upstairs so I ran outside and when I got to the truck, Aubie started peppering me with questions. That's when I got scared! All I could think of was getting the hell outta there. I didn't think of nothing else, I swear. I mean, if I'd've planned it, wouldn't't've gone so smooth. [*She sighed and rubbed her chin over her greasy shoulder.*] Course, try to tell the cops that. How it was just one of those crazy things that just happened. And then I couldn't just ditch her in the middle of nowhere and then, after a while, Aubie was getting such a crush on her that when I'd tell him to stop the truck so I could leave her off someplace, he'd just keep on going. He wouldn't listen to me.

93

VANISHED
by Mary McGarry Morris
Massachusetts - Present - Dotty (20's)

Dotty finds Carl molesting her seven-year-old "daughter." She tries to kill him with a shovel. Then she tells a story about another young girl (herself).

DOTTY: Son of a bitch, [*she said through the cigarette she was lighting.*] Doesn't deserve to live. [*She took a deep drag that wheezed in her chest. For a moment she stared into space.*] Some don't, you know. Once I knew this girl. She was just a kid, really. Fourteen, I think she said. She never had nothing. All her life, nothing. Not even her own bed. Her daddy was just the meanest cocksucker around. I mean, *mean!* [*She shivered and hugged herself.*] He was always at her. Just all the time, every minute on her case. 'Do this! Don't do that! Help your Ma! Take them kids out for a walk!' He never let her be a little kid herself, you know what I mean? Him and her mother, they just used her. Only he was the worse; he used her the worse way of all. First, it was touching. Then, it was all the way. Poor kid. She was only ten and then when she was thirteen, she went to her Ma and told her. And her Ma said, 'You dirty, lying, pig tramp, saying such things about your own Daddy.'

And her Ma slapped her and punched her and kicked her and just went crazy, beating on her and screaming, 'Pig tramp, dirty little pig tramp....' Beat her so bad she couldn't go to school for a week till the sores and cuts got better. So then this girl I knew said, 'I'll fix her! I'll show her!' And she waited till just the right time, till he was drunk and half mean and half sexed up and winking and rubbing himself against the corner of the table and getting that blindy look he'd get like a flabby-donked old bull, tryna talk sweet, but only could think of dirty words like a little kid.

Only that time she didn't steer clear of him. She didn't leave the house or the room even. Her Ma was due home from cleaning the pigman's place any minute and all her little sisters were on the floor

94

watching TV. She sat up on the chair staring down at the backs of their heads and she thought how if somebody didn't do something, if somebody didn't stop him, then he'd be on one of them next, on one of those sweet little girls she loved so much like they were her own even. So she just sat there and let him keep on and keep on and keep on. And so just when she figured it was time for her Ma to get there, she looked up at him and she smiled and, for the first time, she didn't try to run or anything.

He grabbed her and she just got up and never once pulled back and went in the room there and never said a word. He was just getting ready and she heard the shed door open and close and then she heard her Ma's voice saying hello to her little sisters. Right then he started on her and once he got going, he didn't care if the whole county came by. 'Ma!' she hollered. 'Ma! Come and get him off me. Ma! Help me, Ma!'

And you know what happened then? [*Dotty smiled, almost amusedly.*] The TV just got louder and louder and louder and then she just stopped screaming and fighting and just laid there and waited for him to finish. And she knew then how it was the same for her Ma in a way. How it was up to her, she knew, to keep him off all of them.

After that, if she said anything, all her Ma ever said was, 'I can't do nothing. Run away then. Take off.' And by then she had a boy she liked, this older guy she used to tell about her and her Daddy to, only she said how it was someone else she knew. And this guy said, 'Tell your friend, some bastards don't deserve to live.'

And then one night, right after that, it was a boiling hot night and she was sleeping on the couch with just a shirt on and in he came in the middle of the night. It was so hot and sticky and, to tell the truth, she was kinda high herself and had just a while before snuck in from her date with the guy she liked; and he kept shaking her, tryna wake her up, and just when he was gonna lay on her, she rolled off the couch and ran outside, and he took off after her with his bottle in his hand. He caught her, and when it was over, he sat

VANISHED

up and lit a cigarette and took a swig, and all of a sudden she
grabbed the bottle and she just let him have it. Over and over on his
head and his face, and when the bottle was just the broken neck left
with blood in her hand, she picked up a big rock and kept on going.
Then, just so there wouldn't be any doubt, so her Ma'd know, so
everyone'd know, so he'd know, she lit a match and tried to set him
on fire there. The matches kept going out but she could smell his
hair burning. So she kept lighting them, one after the other, till the
book was empty.

[*Dotty looked at the cigarette she was stubbing out in the litter
of potato chips and ashes.*] The weird thing is, she wanted more
matches. That's all she could think of, how she needed more
matches. But when she got back to the house, the door was locked.
So she slept in the shed and then, the next morning, he didn't come
back, so she knew he was dead. When her Ma left for the pigman's,
she got more matches and went back and tore off his shirt sleeves
and put them on his belly and lit them, but the fire kept going out.
So she figured she better get going, only she got lost in the woods
that day and night and maybe even the next. And she could hear
men's voices, sounding mean and hot and mad, and she could hear
dogs baying and snarling, and she knew they weren't gonna listen.
It hit her how it was probably gonna be just like all those times with
her Ma. They'd call her dirty names and they'd never believe her.

97

99